Mushrooms

Jane Eastoe

Mushrooms

A guide to collecting and cooking mushrooms

 National Trust

First published in the United Kingdom in 2011 by
National Trust Books
10 Southcombe Street
London W14 0RA

An imprint of Anova Books Company Ltd

ISBN 9781907892042

A CIP catalogue for this book is available from the British Library.

16 15 14 13 12 11
10 9 8 7 6 5 4 3 2 1

Repro by Mission Productions Ltd, Hong Kong.
Printed and bound by Everbest, China.

This book can be ordered direct from the publisher at the website www.anovabooks.com,
or try your local bookshop. Also available at National Trust shops.

ACKNOWLEDGEMENTS

Thanks go to my husband Eric who, despite initial reservations, now
confidently consumes my foraged mushrooms. He also provides a fabulous
dictionary service when my spelling fails me and can always be relied
upon to resolve grammatical queries. I must also thank my daughter
Florence for her superb proof-reading skills and for her enthusiasm,
encouragement and good-natured compliance in testing the many recipes
in this book. Unusually my son Teddy has been of little help, but can be
forgiven in this instance as he has a pathological hatred of mushrooms.
My stepdaughter Genevieve has been a superb assistant on foraging forays,
many gastronomic treats would have been missed without her eagle-eyes.
Finally I would like to thank Polly Powell, Tina Persaud and Lucy Smith
for their support, and for their faith in me.

CONTENTS

A NOTE ON CONSERVATION   6

INTRODUCTION   8

THE BIOLOGY   16

THE HUNT   22

COOKING   30

DIRECTORY OF FUNGI   49

USEFUL ORGANISATIONS   92

BIBLIOGRAPHY   94

INDEX   96

A NOTE ON CONSERVATION

Edible qualities aside, fungi are immensely valuable. They clear up rotting and dead organic material, recycling it to become productive soil. They provide and transport essential nutrients to many trees and plants. Thus, any deterioration in the variety, quantity or quality of fungi within a landscape will impact on the health of that ecosystem. Understanding this is key to being an informed, responsible and safe forager.

CODE OF CONDUCT

Before you begin fungi foraging you must be *au fait* with the code of conduct.

- Always seek permission from the landowner.
- Remember it is illegal to collect fungi from SSSIs (Sites of Special Scientific Interest) and on most nature reserves.
- Follow the Countryside Code in England and Wales, or the Scottish Outdoor Access Code, drawn up to protect the environment. Another valuable code to follow is The Wild Mushroom Pickers' Code at www.bms.ac.uk/Code.html
- Take a guide book with you and try to identify the fungi *in situ* before picking.
- Do not collect any fungi that you do not intend to eat and only collect from a plentiful supply. Ecosystems depend on fungi for food and protection from disease, so please only ever take a small proportion of a single type from any area, particularly in ancient woodland.It is worth considering that picking one or two may be causing considerable damage to

an entire species – particularly when picking bracket fungi such as Beefsteak and Cauliflower Fungus, Chicken of the Woods and Hedgehog Mushroom – so it is important to check with an expert.

- Do not pick button mushrooms. Collect only mushrooms that have opened – this way not only do you get bigger mushrooms, but you also allow the spores to be discharged.
- Don't pick mushrooms from busy roadsides where they will have been exposed to pollution, or from fields that may have been sprayed with pesticides.
- The foraging advice given in this book is for personal consumption. The National Trust does not condone picking for commercial use, which can incur heavy fines.

Increased interest in foraging has provoked some concern among ecologists. Epping Forest, a favoured haunt for collectors in autumn, is home to 1,600 species of wild mushroom. The Corporation of London, which owns and manages it, used to turn a blind eye to foragers, then moved on to a system of licensing and more recently has begun enforcing a complete ban, with anyone caught picking mushrooms now liable for prosecution. Epping Forest is an SSSI and the Corporation has been forced to take this action because illegal picking had reached record highs and was threatening the diversity of fungi found there. In one weekend alone 45kg (100lb) of mushrooms were confiscated.

Both the Association of British Fungus Groups and the British Mycological Society run extremely popular and informative courses at National Trust properties across the UK. These forays are led by experts and you will get great advice on identification.Visit www.nationaltrust.org.uk for further details.

INTRODUCTION

Wild fungi, gourmet treats beloved by chefs of distinction, are there for the picking for a good nine months of the year in the UK. Blessed with the most exquisite and distinctive flavours – yet capable of killing you stone dead if you make an error in identification – wild fungi and the hunt for them are regarded here at best as a hazardous pastime and at worst as a threat to our woodland ecosystem. No such attitudes dominate in Europe, where wild fungi are sold in local markets and expert advice as to what is safe and what is not, is readily at hand.

In her book *An Omelette and a Glass of Wine*, Elizabeth David details the extraordinary range of wild fungi offered for sale in the Italian town of Alba: '… there are baskets of prime mushrooms to look at and to smell, chestnut and ochre coloured *funghi porcini*, the cèpes or *Boletus edulis* common in the wooded countryside of Piedmont, and some fine specimens of the beautiful red-headed *Amanita caesara*, the young of which are enclosed in an egg-shaped white cocoon, or volva, which has earned them the name of *funghi uovali*, egg mushrooms. They are the *oronges* considered by some French fungi-fanciers as well as by the Piedmontese to be the best of all mushrooms.'

So why is there is more nervousness about collecting fungi in the UK than any other form of wild food? It is as though we are infected with an irrational and all-encompassing fear. I blame all those lurid fairytales from childhood: virtually every fantastic illustration hints at danger with a liberal sprinkling of red-and-white spotted toadstools – often squatted by a vindictive sprite. No wonder we instinctively back away when we come across them in a wood. Yet wild mushrooms, of all forms of wild food, can offer some of the most perfect taste experiences and are lauded by such culinary luminaries as Antonio Carluccio, Hugh Fearnley-Whittingstall and the late Jane Grigson.

TOADSTOOLS OR MUSHROOMS?

Myths abound on how to discern the difference between a 'mushroom' and a 'toadstool', despite there being no actual technical difference. It is generally accepted that the term 'toadstool' applies to anything that is poisonous and/or umbrella shaped, while the term 'mushroom' is reserved for some, but not all, edible fungi, notably those in the *Agaricus* family which contains such gourmet delights as the Field Mushroom (*Agaricus campestris*) and the Horse Mushroom (*A. arvensis*), but also the malicious Yellow Stainer (*A. xanthodermus*) Therefore, for the purposes of this book, the term toadstool is not used at all, while the terms mushroom and fungus are used interchangeably.

THE HISTORY OF EATING WILD FUNGI

You could attempt to blame the apparent British indifference to wild fungi on the shift from rural to urban living over the course of the Industrial Revolution. In 1801 only one-fifth of the population lived in towns and cities, but by 1901 the ratio was reversed, with four-fifths residing in the cities – and much of our rural heritage was lost in the process. The truth is that the British, unlike the French, Italians, Swiss, Germans, Poles and Russians, have always been reluctant to utilise this seasonal fare. The knowledge of which fungi could be safely gathered from the woods, fields and hedgerows was never passed down from parent to child as it was in rural Europe, nor was a system of inspection introduced to help collectors identify their finds, such as is found in France, Italy and Switzerland.

In 1910 The British Board of Agriculture published a booklet, *Edible and Poisonous Fungi*, containing 25 coloured plates designed to educate the British population; it was a tacit acknowledgement that the situation was entirely different on the continent where no such encouragement was required. Bulletin No. 23 ran into several editions; the final two were printed in 1940 and 1945 in an effort to introduce Britain under rationing to a potential food source.

More recently there has been a surge of interest in the subject, even the supermarkets are stocking more than the basic *Agaricus bisporus*, the cultivated mushroom that dominates the commercial market in button, closed-cup and open-cup form. Now oyster mushrooms and porcini are readily available –

albeit the latter mainly in dried form – but even they only hint at the delicacies that await the successful forager.

This book aims to start you off in the process of safely and *responsibly* identifying, collecting and cooking wild mushrooms. If you want to enjoy them then you first have to learn how to identify them reliably. There are many more edible wild varieties than there are poisonous ones, though some, while safe to eat, have nothing notable in the flavour department to recommend them. Not that I am proposing that you give fungi collecting a shot on the basis that you are more likely to pick a safe one than a poisonous one. The odds may be stacked in your favour but this would be a form of foraging Russian roulette.

FORAGING

There are several schools of thought on how to teach people to hunt for wild mushrooms. A common approach is to begin by teaching identification of the most deadly and toxic mushrooms, for this is a hobby that can, if not treated responsibly or taken seriously, kill. Golfing, fly-fishing, kite flying and any number of hobbies don't have as many potentially lethal associations as the consumption of wild fungi – but neither do they offer the same wild excitement or number of free gourmet dinners that fungi foraging does.

The problem with first learning to identify the most dangerous mushrooms is that the hunter can lose enthusiasm for the subject. I personally believe that a more user-friendly approach is to start by learning what you *can* safely eat with impunity; there are a number of delicious mushrooms that even the beginner can collect with the confidence that the experiment will not end up in the morgue – or perhaps more likely, hanging over the toilet bowl. Please do remember that the safest way to forage is with an expert guide.

Some fungi can make you very ill indeed. Some can kill you. Some species can be eaten and regarded as a great delicacy by some people, but the same mushroom will give other people an upset stomach. Some mushrooms are edible only when they have been cooked to destroy the toxins they contain. When eating any mushroom for the first time always cook it first and eat only a small piece in case of adverse reaction.

INDENTIFICATION: START FROM SCRATCH

Ditch any rules that your Auntie Muriel, or the landlord of the local pub have passed on. There is no easy route to fungi identification, no one rule that serves as an all-encompassing health and safety guarantee. Here are some common misconceptions: anything with pink gills is safe – wrong; anything that changes colour when cut is poisonous – wrong; all mushrooms coloured blue or green are toxic – wrong; if it smells like a mushroom you can eat it – wrong; if it has been nibbled then all mammals can eat it – wrong; if the cap can be peeled you can eat it – wrong! Dismiss *all* generalisations and go back to the basics of identification.

It is very important that you learn how to recognise the different species. Remember, even these can vary in appearance from the textbook description due to age or the environment. Mushroom hunting is a very safe hobby so long as you never, ever, consume a mushroom that you cannot identify with 100 per cent certainty – a *laissez-faire* attitude can leave you very poorly indeed.

Nicholas Evans, author of *The Horse Whisperer*, perfectly illustrates the need for caution and vigilance. In 2008 he, and members of his family, famously picked a good pound or so of wild fungi while on holiday in Scotland, which they cooked and ate for lunch. Evans had collected wild mushrooms before with no ill-effects, unfortunately in this instance the party mistook Deadly Web Caps for Ceps and only consulted a guidebook after they had consumed the mushrooms. Two days later Evans, his wife, his brother-in-law and sister-in-law were in hospital, critically ill, with their kidneys under attack from the chemical orellanine. They were lucky not to die and all bar Evan's sister-in-law, still have to have dialysis and are on the waiting list for kidney transplants.

OTHER HAZARDS

Newspapers in Italy recently reported that 18 people died in 2010 alone as a result of the nation's passion for wild mushrooms – though they died not from eating wild mushrooms, but from falling down mountains while collecting them. The message is clear: if we learn to identify edible mushrooms, the most danger we face from collecting them is accidentally tripping up! This book will teach you how to identify edible mushrooms. The donning of sensible footwear I leave to you.

This is not a handbook for mycologists – those who make a study of fungi. It is designed to be a user-friendly introduction to edible mushrooms: where you can find them, how to safely identify them, as well as how best to cook them and store them for future use. It is not a fully comprehensive study of the subject, there are many, many more edible wild fungi than I have listed here, but then any mushroom hunter, or indeed mycologist, will tell you that one book alone is never enough. This book is designed to get you off the starting block and out into the woods, safely collecting fungi for your supper or breakfast. Before you know it you'll have a shelf of fungi books to consult, all of which have their place in the identification process. Listed here are some of the most important culinary mushrooms and some of the safest and easiest to find.

It is also important that the novice hunter appreciates that no amount of textbook reading, however good or extensive the book, can replace practical experience with a friendly guide. There are field courses available around the country; many are supported by local authorities.

Alternatively you can go to the British Mycological Society, the Association of British Fungus Groups, or the Wildlife Trust for advice on where to find a course. No special equipment is required to gather mushrooms, but a knife for cutting, a brush to remove excess leaf or soil matter on site, and a trug to transport your precious cargo, won't go amiss – especially if you want to look the part.

It won't take long for you to be confident about recognising the most delicious edible mushrooms – a skill that you can then pass down from generation to generation. None of us thinks twice about collecting blackberries from the hedgerow; collecting edible fungi can equally become second nature, even if you stick to only a few foolproof species.

A book on fungi entitled *Britain's Wild Larder* and published more than 50 years ago (see Bibliography p.94) held out the optimistic notion that one day British collectors would routinely have their finds checked by inspectors, as occurs in Europe. That day is still a long way off, but educating yourself is the next best option.

THE BIOLOGY

Fungi are a distinct group of living organisms, entirely separate from the animal and plant kingdom. The spectrum ranges from micro-organisms such as moulds and yeasts, through to 'higher fungi' or mushrooms. Fungi can be found in soil, on plants, in the air and water, even on the human body. They can cause discomfort and disease: Candida, *commonly known as thrush, and* Trichophyton rubrum *or athlete's foot, are two common fungal infections. Fungi can also save our lives: penicillin and other antibiotics are made from fungi. And without fungi we would not have some of the staples of life such as bread, cheese or beer.*

Fungi serve a fundamental role in the environment; they break down material to provide rich soil. The sheer quantity and bulk of cellulose that fungi quietly and thanklessly decompose is almost beyond belief and it is this process that restores nutrients to the soil. It is thought that only five to ten per cent of plants survive without the assistance of fungi, and they have an essential symbiotic relationship with woodland.

THE UNDERGROUND BODY

The mushroom is the fruiting body of the fungi, its reproductive organs if you like. The actual 'body' of the fungi – the mycelium – is threading its way quietly through the ground or the wood beneath it, entirely out of sight. Mycelium is made up of filaments called hyphae, finer than a cobweb and so minute that they are invisible to the naked eye.

Hyphae often travel several metres to maintain the mycelium's supply of nutrients. The Fairy Ring Champignon grows in rings that indicate the size of the mycelium below; an example in eastern France with a diameter of nearly 1 km (⅝ mile) is reputed to be some 700 years old.

SIZE MATTERS

Do not underestimate the size that fungi can reach. The largest known living organism is the Honey Mushroom (*Armillaria ostoyae*) which starts, as all do, from a single spore and spreads and spreads and spreads. Found in the Malheur National Forest in Oregon, USA, the outline of the biggest specimen stretches for 5.6 kilometres (3.5 miles) and extends downwards an average of 1 metre (3ft) into the ground. DNA tests established that this one mighty organism covers an area of 1,665 football pitches. It cannot be seen as it spreads underground, but its fruit pop up all over the area.

TYPES OF FUNGI

Fungi do not contain chlorophyll – the pigment in plants that allows them to use the sun's energy. Instead they absorb nutrients directly from animal or vegetable sources. We tend to think of fungi as being parasitic; in fact there are three types; saprophytic, mycorrhizal and parasitic. Saprophytes live on dead and dying organic matter – leaf mould, tree stumps, fallen timber on the ground and so on. Mycorrhizal fungi have a mutually beneficial relationship with the roots of certain plants and trees; the fungi assist water and nutrient uptake, receiving sugars in return. Some of our most prized culinary fungi such as Truffles and Boletes are mycorrhizal. This symbiotic relationship is very difficult to reproduce in cultivation, ensuring that these wild fungi maintain their prized status. Parasitic fungi do as you would expect and live off their host to its detriment. Classic examples are the Honey Fungus, familiar to many in the UK, its appearance heralding the death of a tree or shrub, and the Honey Mushroom, cited above, which destroys forests.

FRUITING BODIES

Fungi do not produce 'fruit' until they have colonised the soil or plant material they are living on. When environmental conditions are suitable they will send out the fruit or reproductive organs. This stage varies but typically in a mushroom such as *Agaricus*, the hyphae mesh to form a white lump under the soil surface which, as it grows, begins to move upwards on a developing stalk. When the fruit body breaks through the soil in its 'button' phase it is encased by sheath of tissue known as the veil. Inside, the cap and gills are developing, but as the cap expands and starts to move outwards into an umbrella shape the veil tears and the gills are exposed. The remnants of the veil leave a ring on the stalk, but this is not present in all fungi species.

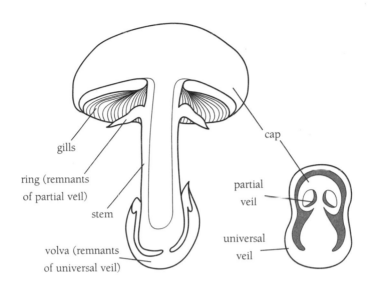

gills

ring (remnants
of partial veil)

stem

volva (remnants
of universal veil)

cap

partial
veil

universal
veil

Mature fruit body   **Developing fruit body**

The *Amanita* family, which includes the red and white
'toadstool' (Fly Agaric) of children's picture books, has a
double skinned veil: remnants of one cling to the cap
producing the legendary warty spots; the other leaves tattered
remnants around the stem to form the characteristic ring. At
the base of the *Amanita* stem is a bag known as the volva from
which the cap erupted, tearing through the veil.

REPRODUCTION

Fungi do not produce seeds, but propagate themselves by means of spores in enormous quantities; a single Giant Puffball is reputed to generate seven billion – though only a tiny proportion will succeed in spawning. These tiny particles, no bigger than dust, are dispensed in a variety of ways. Most are launched like mini-rockets from their gill base and are distributed by wind, rain or insects. Each spore is theoretically capable of germinating into a hypha, which in turn grows and develops until it forms the mycelium.

The method by which the spores are dispensed is used to classify fungi. There are three principal groups. The *Ascomycetes* or sac fungi, form spores in small sacs called asci, the classic example being the Morel. The *Basidiomycetes* or spore droppers form spores on short stalks attached to club-shaped bodies (basidia), usually on gills or pores under the cap. This group includes many different types of mushroom, such as Boletes, Agarics, and Jelly Fungus. The third group, the *Zygomycetes*, includes fungi such as bread moulds, whose fruiting bodies cannot usually be seen with the naked eye.

TOXINS

We do not yet understand why some fungi can be safely eaten, while others produce lethal toxins or alkaloids with hallucinogenic properties. The toxins do not affect all animals as they do humans; rabbits dine on the Death Cap (*Amanita phalloides*) with apparent impunity, their systems being able to neutralise the toxins. Bunnies aside, the genus *Amanita* contains some of the most vicious toxins and is held to be responsible for most human deaths from mushroom poisoning throughout the world. I have it on great authority that the appropriately named Destroying Angel (*Amanita virosa*) tastes delicious, but I do not intend to sample even the smallest piece myself to test the theory and urge you to show similar restraint. This lethal fungi spreads its poison through the body with great discretion – by the time the toxins make their presence felt it may well be too late for treatment to be effective. Those admitted to hospital some 60 hours after ingestion have a 50–90 per cent mortality rate.

Here are a few more examples of mycotoxins (toxins produced by a fungus): muscarine isn't necessarily deadly, but it can cause respiratory failure; alpha-amanitin, which is the main toxin in *Amanita* leads to fatal liver damage, as does orrellanine; gyromitrin affects the neurotransmitters and can lead to tremors or seizures as well as causing the red blood cells to break down. And that's without the many other toxins that can lead to vomiting, diarrhoea, hallucination, dizziness, confusion – among a myriad of other serious side-effects.

I freely acknowledge that for the first year or two when I began to collect wild mushrooms to eat, a certain unease would descend as I contemplated my gourmet treat, no matter how obsessively I had checked and rechecked my identification. I inevitably suffered a little indigestion later and would wonder if I could possibly have made a fatal error. But as your confidence increases, this nervous indigestion goes, and repeated forays year after year to tried and tested spots demonstrate that foraging for fungi is a deeply pleasurable and perfectly safe pastime.

THE HUNT

While autumn with its mists and mellow fruitfulness is indisputably the time of year when mushrooms are most abundant, do not fall into the trap of thinking that this is the only time to go collecting. Many delicacies appear at other times of the year. In spring you can hunt for the St George's Mushroom, the Fairy Ring Champignon, the Field Mushroom and the divine Morel. In summer you can look for Chanterelles, the Parasol Mushroom, the Saffron Milk Cap and Chicken of the Woods. While in winter there are the Blewits and Trumpet Chanterelles, and the likes of Jelly Ear and the Oyster Mushroom can be found all year round.

WEATHER AND SEASON

The weather and the seasons are key pointers for hunters. While fungi need moisture to fruit, it is not a good idea to hunt either in the rain or immediately after a long period of wet weather. In such conditions many fungi become waterlogged and slimy and those that are still worth collecting will decay faster than those collected in dry weather. Besides, there is nothing nicer than collecting mushrooms on a sunny autumn day – it is one of life's great pleasures. Mushrooms can be found for around nine months of the year: January, February, March and much of April tend to be barren months and September and October the most fruitful.

The season in which a mushroom appears is another key identification factor. For example, you simply will not find a Morel in autumn – as I discovered when my elation on finding a curiously ghostly white Morel one September was diminished by the realisation, having consulted various field guides, that my 'Morel' was in fact nothing but a foetid Stinkhorn. September and October finds many fungi species fruiting and the first frosts stop them in their tracks.

EQUIPMENT

Use a firm container to hold your fungi – an open basket or trug is ideal and you can use dry leaves to stop your finds rolling around or banging into each other. Plastic bags are a bad idea as the fungi can bruise and sweat, and equally cloth bags and net bags do not offer much protection.

Don't be disconcerted if when you first start hunting you can't see any fungi at all – it can take a little time to get your eye in. You need to hunt carefully; the little blighters hardly ever sprout conveniently close to the path. Many will hide among the undergrowth, or disguise themselves among fallen leaves. At first you may only find masses of little brown mushrooms that defy identification, save by the experienced mycologist. It's incredibly helpful to take children along; they are remarkably adept at spotting fungi and become hugely enthusiastic at all the different types that they can find – a whole new world uncovered at their feet. Just don't let them taste their finds until they've been identified and taken home and cooked.

HOW TO PICK

Remove fungi by twisting them gently out of the ground – don't use a knife to cut them as this can introduce disease to the mycelium below. However a knife is useful to help you gently prise specimens out of the ground intact – it will also help to ensure that you can see the base of the stem, which is especially helpful in identifying dangerous *Amanita*. An exception to the rule can be made in the case of fungi growing in trees, as these do not simply pull away and need to be cut off. Please ensure you check with the landowner before taking these specimens.

Only collect mushrooms that have opened; immature mushrooms in their 'button' stage do not reveal enough characteristics for safe identification. By the same token, old mushrooms can become infested with insects and decay rapidly and are best left alone. Maggots are the mushroom collector's nemesis, and you must examine your haul carefully to ensure that you do not get more protein than you bargained for. I once left a mushroom I was attempting to identify on one side for 48 hours; looking for it later I was amazed to discover that it had vanished, leaving a pile of squirming maggots in its place! What you are looking for is young, firm, whole specimens: anything that is bruised, soggy, infested or over-ripe should be left alone to drop its spores.

IDENTIFICATION

The shape, texture, colour and perfume of the mushroom, along with the appearance of its gills (some fungi have tubes and pores instead of gills) and spore colour are significant aides to identification. You also need to take into account the time of year, and the location. Note whether it is growing in a ring and what is growing nearby – many species of mushroom will only grow near certain types of tree. Even if you cannot precisely identify specific fungi, you will quickly learn to recognise what family it is from and your knowledge will expand with practise and experience.

Please do not get disheartened when you first try your hand at identification; fungi are much harder to tell apart than plants. The detail that differentiates one from another is often small. However, there are a few species that are comparatively easy to recognise and safe to eat because they have no toxic look-alikes: most notable are the Giant Puffball, the Cep, the Shaggy Inkcap, the Morel, the Jelly Ear, the Hedgehog Fungus and the Cauliflower Fungus.

Each component of the mushroom has a set of characteristics that will enable you to tell it apart from its relatives. While I have tried to steer away from the use of technical terms in this book, I will highlight them here to enable you to understand the minute technical details that make all the difference in becoming familiar with a range of species.

THE CAP

The colour is a great starting point, but in mushroom identification there are nuances of shade. When you start everything will look like a small buff mushroom, but tan is different from beige, and a pinky cream different from grey.

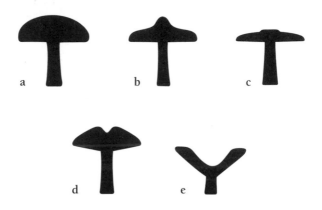

Looking at the cap in profile its shape can be: convex (a),
fairly straightforward in having a curved outline; umbonate
(b), having a central curved lump; gibbous (c), with a
flattened central hump; umbilicate (d), having a central
depression; and infundibuliform (e), meaning funnel shaped.
There are, of course, perfectly round fungi such as the Giant
Puffball, an outsize sphere that is hard to miss.

The cap can be smooth in texture: some feel as soft and dry as
chamois leather, others are greasy or sticky. It can have warty,
scaly or fringed flesh. Some fungi drip a fluid: the Beefsteak
Fungus oozes a red, blood-like fluid from its meaty body. The
flesh of a fungus can undergo distinct and startling colour
changes when bruised or cut with a knife.

THE GILLS

Note the shape of the gills – the flat slivers under the cap –
and their density; they can be described as distant when they
are widely spaced, or crowded when they are close together.
The profile of the gills and how they are attached to the cap is
also revealing, as is the colour. The profile of the gills can be
described as: free, that is, not connected to the stem; adnexed,
connected to the stem by a portion of the gill – sometimes just
touching; adnate indicates that the whole depth of the gill is
attached to the stem, as can be seen in *Russulas* (see pages 53
and 62); sinuate has a gill that curves inward to the stem so
that it is notched or hooked where it attaches; decurrent gills
run down a portion of the stem, as seen in the Chanterelle.

Not all fungi have gills. Some have tubes that house the spore-
producing layer, such as the Cep or the Beefsteak Fungus. In
this book I refer to the tubes as pores – the pore is technically
the mouth of the tube, which is what you see on the
underside. Another arrangement occurs in fungi such as the
Hedgehog Fungus, which has tiny, fragile spines – or teeth –
that hang down a few millimetres or more; there are few
mushrooms within this group so it is a straightforward
identifying feature.

If you rub the gills with your finger you may well see a dark
smudge – this is the spores, though obviously if they are white
or pink they will be less noticeable. The best way of
determining the spore colour is to take a spore print. It takes
about ten seconds to set up and I maintain it is one of the
great miracles of nature. Cut off the stalk and pop the cap on
to a piece of paper. Place an upturned glass over the top to

stop air movement affecting the print. Leave in place for about 12 hours – overnight is ideal, though you can get faster results when the mushroom is fresh – then lift off the glass and the mushroom. You will uncover a piece of artwork: the shape of the gills delineated perfectly and the colour of the spore print revealed. Some fungi have white or very pale spores, so to obtain a good print use black paper instead of white. Every child should take a spore print once in their life – they will be astonished by the result. A spore print is a reliable determining factor in species that are hard to tell one from the other.

Illustration of spore print

THE STEM

The stem is revealing in shape, colour, markings, texture and the presence or absence of a ring or perhaps a bag at the base. It can be hollow, solid, or filled with cottony fibres. In shape it is most commonly cylindrical, spindle shaped – that is, lumpy in the middle – or stout at the base. It can have a fibrous or smooth surface.

PERFUME

A final note on perfume. Most mycologists agree that the smells of various mushrooms are a significant aid to identification. Chanterelles are commonly described as smelling of apricots and the Horse Mushroom of aniseed, but any analysis of a perfume is very much a personal assessment. I have to confess that most fungi smell plain mushroomy to me, but it doesn't stop me collecting.

COOKING

Cooking mushrooms is simplicity itself, though there are a few tricks that will make it easier. In addition, if you have a very large haul (no more than 1.5kg/3.5lb), fungi can be preserved, a process explained later in this chapter. However, I would urge you to collect only what you can eat fresh. My reasoning is twofold: firstly it is the exquisite taste and the range of textures found in fresh wild fungi that makes their consumption such a gourmet experience. Secondly, over-picking is seriously bad news for all fungi collectors; if we take only what we can eat fresh within 24 hours, we leave plenty behind to spore.

Wild fungi do not stay at their best for long. Aim to eat anything you have found within a day of picking. If you have transported them gently, in an open rigid container and not in a plastic bag, then they should be in good condition. When you get home check each fungus carefully: if you are not one hundred per cent certain that this is the mushroom you think it is, bin it. Store the fungi in a cool place until required and spread them out so that they do not touch.

PREPARATION

When you are ready to cook, examine each fungus. A delicious edible mushroom can still make you ill if you do not eat it when it is fresh. We do not eat meat when it is old, nor should we eat wild fungi past their 'best by' date. Similarly make sure that your haul is not riddled with maggots, or any other undesirable squatters. Check the base of the stalk for holes and trim the end. Look out for bruising; sometimes the affected segment can be cut away, or if the pores have become a little soggy they can be cut away and just the flesh utilised – for example, when preparing a Bolete.

Never clean mushrooms until you are ready to use them. Wherever possible use a brush to tease out dirt from between the gills, or wipe them with a damp cloth. If they require washing do this at the last possible moment, as quickly as possible, one at a time. Leave them to drain in a colander, then pop them on a piece of kitchen roll or a cloth to absorb more of the water. Never leave freshly picked fungi to soak in a bowl of water as they will lose some of their flavour. Most wild mushrooms do not require peeling – utilise every morsel.

Don't ever eat a wild mushroom raw until you have checked that it is safe to eat uncooked; some delicious edible fungi contain toxins that are destroyed in the cooking process (rather like cooking nettles in soup) and therefore rendered safe, but will make you feel poorly eaten *au naturel*; others are safe to eat in salads.

If you are following a recipe from a book that doesn't specify using wild mushrooms then you may be able to reduce the required quantities, as cultivated mushrooms are far less flavourful than their wild relations.

The trick to sautéing mushrooms successfully is to do so with a mix of olive oil and butter in equal proportions. Butter burns easily and the addition of oil helps to prevent this. Most mushrooms release a lot of fluid as they cook, though inevitably there are some exceptions to the rule; continue cooking them gently until this fluid has evaporated, to concentrate the flavour. If there is so much liquid that it is taking too long to evaporate, then drain a little off. Don't forget seasoning; a good helping of salt and pepper really brings out that wonderful flavour. Add seasoning while there is still plenty of liquid in the pan, allowing the mushrooms time to absorb it.

DRYING

If you collect too many mushrooms, or you cannot use them as planned, don't let them go to waste; it is very easy to dry mushrooms for future use, although not all specimens are suitable. Sort through your haul and use only the best of the bunch – specimens that are free from insects and bruising. Clean and dry them as necessary; slice if large, leave whole if small; then lay them on a piece of paper or a wire rack and leave somewhere warm, such as the airing cupboard, for a few days. Some people run a thread through the stems and suspend their fungal 'bunting' over the radiator to dry. There are also some glorious Heath Robinson-style contraptions involving roles of wire and giant fans, but these are hardly required for drying just a few specimens. If you are into gadgets, a food dehydrator will do the job efficiently for you.

When the mushrooms are completely dry, store them in airtight jars as they are, or put them in a food processor first, until you have finely chopped mushrooms for flavouring casseroles and soups. When you want to use the mushrooms place them in a bowl of hot water for at least half an hour: don't throw this water away when the process is complete, it is packed with flavour.

Not all mushrooms dry well. It is one of life's great tragedies that the divine Chanterelle is not a suitable candidate; it retains its golden colour, but the flesh is rendered tasteless and tough. Any Bolete dries beautifully; the Penny Bun is, after all, the fresh version of the prized porcini that features in so many recipes – so if you have a glut, don't let them go to waste. Similarly the Morel dries and reconstitutes very well, plus it is prohibitively expensive to purchase dried (and fresh). The Horn of Plenty, Jelly Ear, Fairy Ring Champignon and the Cauliflower Fungus also dry beautifully.

RECIPES

MUSHROOM SOUP

Serves 4–6

50g (2oz) dried porcini
25g (1oz) butter
1 large onion, finely diced
2 cloves of garlic, crushed
500g (1lb 2oz) mixed wild mushrooms
1 large glass of dry white wine
750ml (1¼ pints) chicken stock (or vegetable)
Salt and pepper
150ml (¼ pint) double cream
Large handful of flat-leaf parsley, finely chopped

This recipe comes from my best friend, ace cook and best-selling author Kate Shirazi – it is so very delicious that even my son, who loathes mushrooms, adores it. Start by covering the dried mushrooms in boiling water and leave them to wallow for 30 minutes. Melt the butter in a large pan and gently soften the onion, without letting it brown. Add the garlic and continue to cook for a minute or two. Add the mushrooms and let them soften and release all their lovely juices. Chuck in the wine, turn up the heat and let the wine bubble away so you are left with about a quarter of the liquid. Then add the stock and simmer gently for ten minutes.

Liquidise the soup in batches and if you want a really smooth finish, push it through a fine sieve – though I personally never bother to do this. Return the soup to a clean pan and season well with salt and pepper. Add the cream and gently warm through without letting it boil. At the last minute add the parsley and serve with a flourish.

MUSHROOMS ON TOAST DELUXE

Serves 4

1 onion, finely diced
2 tbsp oil
75g (3oz) butter
450g (1lb) mixed wild mushrooms
1 tsp lemon zest
Half a glass of white wine
150ml (¼ pint) double cream
Handful of fresh parsley, roughly chopped
Black pepper
French loaf cut into slices and crisped in the oven
Grated nutmeg (optional)

My nephew, Jago Coyle, is an awesome cook and this is one of his favourite quick snack lunches, it takes just five minutes to cook and is simply divine. Sweat off the onion in the oil and butter and add the mushrooms, lemon zest and white wine and reduce until the mushrooms start to brown. Then add the double cream until the mushrooms are about half covered.

Chop the parsley roughly and pop into the pan along with plenty of black pepper. Reduce until you have a thick mushroomy sauce, then spoon it over the French bread. A little nutmeg is nice on top if you are a fan.

Serves 4

1.5 litres (2 pints) chicken or vegetable stock
10g (½ oz) dried porcini mushrooms
100g (4oz) butter
450g (1lb) mixed wild mushrooms
4 cloves of garlic, finely chopped
Salt and pepper
1 large onion, finely chopped
3 anchovies, chopped
450g (1lb) risotto (arborio) rice
150ml (¼ pint) dry white wine
40g (1½ oz) Parmesan cheese, grated, plus extra to serve
A sprig of thyme and 1 tbsp fresh thyme leaves (optional)

Susan Espley, one of the best natural cooks I know, makes this risotto, which – unlike some recipes – packs a powerful taste punch. Bring stock and dried porcini to a gentle simmer in a medium saucepan. While this is simmering melt 30g of the butter in a large, heavy-based pan; cook the mushrooms in batches, stirring over a high heat, until softened and browned lightly. Add the garlic, and cook for just a minute or so until fragrant but do not allow it to brown. Season with salt and black pepper. Remove from pan.

Melt 50g of the butter in the same pan. Add the onion, anchovies and sprig of thyme; cook, stirring, until soft but not coloured. Add the rice, stir until the grains are all coated and then stir for a minute. Add the wine and simmer uncovered until the liquid has evaporated.

Remove the stock from the heat and strain. Pour half a cup

of the hot stock into the rice, and cook, stirring over a low
head until the liquid is absorbed. Continue adding the stock
in this way, a little at a time, until it has all been used up – a
process that takes around twenty minutes. Discard the thyme
sprig; stir in the mushrooms, Parmesan, thyme leaves if
desired and remaining butter. Season to taste with salt and
freshly ground black pepper and slivers of Parmesan.

MUSHROOM RAGOUT ON BRIOCHE

Serves 4

2 tbsp olive oil
1 onion, diced
2 cloves of garlic, chopped
2 slices of bacon, finely chopped
450g (1lb) mixed wild mushrooms
10g (½ oz) dried porcini (optional)
275ml (½ pint) red wine
2 tbsp tomato purée
Salt and pepper
4 thick slices of brioche
1 tbsp cornflour
2 handfuls of flat-leaf parsley, roughly chopped
50g (2oz) shaved Pecorino cheese

Heat the oil over medium heat. Add the onion, garlic and
bacon, and cook for five minutes or until the onion is soft and
transparent. Thickly slice all the fresh mushrooms and add
them to the saucepan. Finely chop the dried mushrooms if
using and add them to the pan along with the wine, tomato

purée and a little salt and pepper. Cover with a lid and simmer for forty minutes or until the mushrooms are cooked and the flavours are combined.

Toast the brioche. Meanwhile, put the cornflour in a small bowl with three tablespoons of water and stir until dissolved. Add the cornflour paste to the mushrooms and stir until the mixture has thickened, then remove the pan from the heat. Sprinkle with the chopped parsley.

Place the toasted brioche on four serving plates and top with the mushroom ragout. Top with the shaved Pecorino and serve.

HERB MUSHROOMS

Serves 2

250g (8oz) wild mushrooms; if small leave whole otherwise cut into large chunks
25g (1oz) butter
2 tbsp olive oil
1 clove of garlic
Handful of flat-leaf parsley, chopped
Zest of a lemon

My friend Jaine McCormack, the best vegetarian cook I know, always serves up delicious food in a jiffy, and this mushroom dish is one of my favourites. Fry the mushrooms gently in a mix of butter and olive oil with a little crushed garlic. Add the parsley and lemon zest. Season with salt and black pepper and serve with rice and smoked or roast fish.

CHICKEN AND MUSHROOM PIE

Serves 4–6

3–4 good-size boneless chicken joints or half a leftover
roasted chicken
375g (12oz) shortcrust pastry
250g (8oz) wild mushrooms
1 leek
75g (3oz) butter
300ml (½ pint) cream
375g (12oz) puff pastry
Salt and black pepper
Egg or milk to brush on the pastry

When it comes to making chicken pie, I personally like to use
the leftovers from a roast dinner – it saves another round of
cooking. But if you don't have any then roast the chicken
joints roast in the oven for 40 minutes at 190°C/375°F/Gas
Mark 5, until the flesh is moist and white. Cut the cooked
chicken into small chunks.

Prepare the base of the pie. I confess to being a slave to
ready-made, ready-rolled pastry, if I had to make my own the
family would have very few pies – but don't let me stop you.
Roll out the shortcrust pastry and place in a greased metal pie
tray, approx 25cm/10in in diameter. Prick the base, and cover
with some baking parchment and weigh down with pasta or
rice and bake blind at 150°C/300°F/Gas Mark 2 for about 15
minutes. Remove from the oven and set on one side.

Chop the leek and let it sweat in the butter until softened,
then add the mushrooms and continue to cook gently for
10–15 minutes. Add the cream, chicken pieces and salt and

pepper; continue to cook until the mix is nicely coated, but not too sloppy.

Put the filling into the pie case. Brush the edge of the pastry with milk or egg and then lay the rolled puff pastry on top. Press the edges together and trim. Brush the top with egg or milk and make a few slits in the centre to allow the steam to escape. Bake in an oven at 190°C/375°F/Gas Mark 5 for about 30 minutes until the pie crust is golden brown.

MUSHROOM STROGANOFF

Serves 4

50g (2oz) butter
1 large onion or 3–4 shallots
1 leek
450g (1lb) wild mushrooms
2 tbsp olive oil
1 clove of garlic
2 tsp paprika, or more if you like a stronger taste
1 tbsp brandy (optional)
2 tsp Dijon mustard
Handful of flat-leaf parsley
Squeeze of lemon juice
110ml (4fl oz) vegetable stock
2 tbsp crème fraîche or double cream
Salt and black pepper

Melt the butter in a frying pan then add the oil, chop the onion or shallots and leek and cook until softened, approximately 10–15 minutes. Add the mushrooms, garlic and paprika and cook gently for five minutes, then add the brandy if using – be warned, it may flame. Cook until the liquid has evaporated, then add the lemon juice, mustard and stock and simmer until the liquid is reduced by half. Stir in the crème fraîche and season to taste. Serve on a bed of wild rice or tagliatelle.

POTTED MUSHROOMS

Serves 4

450g (1lb) mixed wild mushrooms
100g (4oz) butter
1 tsp mace
Salt and black pepper

A wonderful lunch recipe or dinner party starter from Kate Shirazi – with the added advantage that it can be made in advance. Clean the mushrooms and tear the big ones into chunks so everything is roughly the same size. Melt half of the butter and chuck the mushrooms in and cook over a medium heat until really soft and beginning to brown. Season with salt and pepper and add the mace. Tip the mushrooms into a sieve and press down to remove as much liquid as possible. Divide the mushrooms into four ramekins, leaving about 2cm (¾in) at the top.

Clarify the rest of the butter by heating it in a pan and letting the white residue sink to the bottom. Carefully pour the clear butter over the the mushrooms, leaving the sediment behind in the pan. Chill until the butter has set and serve with warm toast.

MUSHROOM TART

Serves 4–6

375g (12oz) shortcrust pastry, homemade or shop bought
2–3 shallots
450g (1lb) wild mushrooms
25g (1oz) butter
1 tbsp oil
1 tsp fresh thyme leaves
1 egg plus 1 egg yolk
150ml (¼ pint) double cream
150ml (¼ pint) crème fraîche

This is the perfect dish to show off particularly pretty wild mushrooms. Roll out the pastry and place it in a 25cm (10in) diameter quiche tray. Prick the pastry, cover with baking parchment and weigh down with baking beans (or pasta or rice) and bake blind at 150°C/300°F/Gas Mark 2 for about fifteen minutes.

While the pastry base is baking, chop the shallots finely, cut large mushrooms into segments but leave smaller ones intact. Place the butter and oil in a frying pan and when it is bubbling add the shallots, mushrooms, thyme, salt and pepper. Cook until all the juices have evaporated, then remove from the heat.

Beat the egg and the egg yolk together then add the cream and crème fraîche plus a little salt and pepper and mix together. Put the mushrooms into the pastry shell and spread them out evenly, then pour in the egg and cream mixture. Bake in the oven at 190°C/375°F/Gas Mark 5 for about 30 minutes until the filling is set and taking on colour.

DUXELLES

250g (8oz) wild mushrooms
2 tbsp unsalted butter
3 tbsp chopped shallots
Salt and pepper
1 clove of garlic (optional)
½ tbsp fresh thyme, parsley or chives (optional)
¼ cup white wine or sherry

Duxelles, a sort of mushroom paste, is often used to flavour
soup and stews, and features in the famous dish Beef
Wellington. There are myriad variations, but for me this recipe
is very flavourful and easy to make. Chop the mushrooms
finely, add half of the butter to a non-stick pan and when
melted add the mushrooms, shallots, salt, pepper, garlic if
using, and thyme. Add the remaining butter and when this
has melted add the alcohol. Cook until the liquid has
evaporated. Duxelles can be frozen for future use.

Serves 6–8

1kg (2lb 4oz) of good beef fillet
Salt and black pepper
2 tbsp finely chopped parsley
15g (½ oz) butter
3 tbsp olive oil
500g (1lb 2oz) shortcrust pastry, homemade or shop bought
100g (3oz) coarse liver pâté
A portion of Duxelles (recipe on previous page)
1 beaten egg

A great family friend regularly serves this meal up for dinner on
Boxing Day and, despite over-full tummies, we unapologetically
consume the lot. While the mushrooms are not the star of this
dish, they are an essential part of the whole experience.

Start by seasoning the beef with the salt and pepper
and put on one side for half an hour. Heat the oven to
180°C/350°F/Gas Mark 4.

Roll out the pastry using plenty of flour, making sure that
it is wide and long enough to accommodate the fillet of beef,
if you are using two pieces of pastry allow a good 5cm (2in)
overlap and brush with egg to help keep the pieces together.
Spread the Duxelles mixture over the pastry, leaving a bare
margin all the way around – brush this with beaten egg. Slice
the coarse pâté into tiny slivers and place this on top of the
Duxelles, you won't get complete coverage but dot it around
as best you can. Sprinkle the chopped parsley on top of the
pâté and Duxelles – still keeping the margins clear. Place the
beef on top of the mushroom, pâté and parsley mix and roll it

up in the pastry – trim the ends if there is too much pastry, you want just enough to cover it – and seal. Put a piece of baking parchment on a tray, pop the pastry roll on top of that and brush with the remainder of the beaten egg. Put in the fridge to chill for half an hour – or longer. Bake in the oven for 30–45 minutes until the pastry has turned a beautiful golden colour. Allow it to rest for 5–10 minutes before cutting into thick slices and serving. Ideally the beef will be a little bit pink in the centre, cook for longer if you prefer your meat well done.

MUSHROOM CHOUX BUNS

Serves 4–6

For the choux pastry:
50g (2oz) butter
150ml (¼ pint) water
65g (2½ oz) plain flour
2 eggs, lightly beaten
50g (2oz) Gruyère cheese, finely grated

For the filling:
450g (1lb) mixed wild mushrooms
50g (2oz) butter
1 clove of garlic, crushed
1 glass of white wine
50–100ml (2–4fl oz) cream

Another of Kate Shirazi's life-saving recipes, this makes a wonderfully surprising hors d'oeuvre to pass around on a plate – or serve up as starter. First make the choux buns by putting the butter and the water in a pan and bringing it up to the boil. Take the pan off the heat and quickly chuck in the flour and start beating it with a wooden spoon until it forms a ball in the middle of the pan. Put the pan back on the heat and beat until really smooth. Beat in the eggs a little at a time until the mixture becomes really shiny. Finally, beat in the grated cheese.

Pop dollops of the mixture on to a lined baking tray with plenty of space between them and bake in a hot oven, 220°C/425°F/Gas Mark 7, for 20 minutes or until risen and really golden. Then turn the oven down to 180°C/350°F/Gas

Mark 4. Make a little slit in each bun to let the steam escape and pop them back into the oven for five minutes.

To make the filling, simply fry the mushrooms in the melted butter with the garlic until soft and tinged with brown. Add the wine and let it bubble away to almost nothing. Season well and add enough cream to make a gorgeous sauce that just coats the mushrooms. Fill each hot bun with the warm mushroom mixture and serve, pronto.

PASTA MESS

Serves 4

1 onion, chopped
2 tbsp olive oil
1–2 cloves of garlic, crushed
2 x 400g (13oz) cans of chopped tomatoes
Half a tube of tomato purée
100–150ml (3½–5floz) double cream, according to taste
450g (1lb) mixed wild mushrooms
350g (12oz) penne or other chunky pasta
Salt and pepper
Grated cheese to serve – Parmesan or Cheddar depending on the age of your guests

This is the fond family name for this recipe and one I created myself. My children have eaten it since they were tiny and it is their idea of comfort food. It is not a sophisticated dish, but I once served it up at a smart luncheon in an emergency and it was received with great acclaim. The recipe has been often requested – which I take as a huge compliment. I happily substitute cultivated mushrooms for wild ones when necessary.

Gently simmer the onion in the olive oil until translucent. Add the crushed garlic and cook for a minute or so more, add the chopped tomatoes, tomato purée, the cream and the mushrooms. Bring to a gentle simmer and cook for 15–30 minutes, or more. Season to taste.

Serve up with a chunky pasta and top with grated cheese. This is a fantastic quick dish, but the sauce tastes just as delicious – if not more so – the day after, when the flavour has matured.

Horn of Plenty
(*Craterellus cornucopioides*)

Bay Bolete
(*Boletus badius*)

Field Mushroom
(*Agaricus campestris*)

St Georges Mushroom
(Tricholoma gambosum)

Chanterelle
(Cantharellus cibarius)

Chanterelle
(detail)

Fairy Ring Champignon
(*Marasmius oreades*)

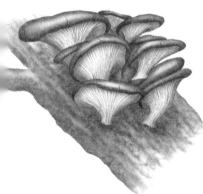

Oyster Mushroom
(*Pleurotus ostreatus*)

Branching Oyster
(*Pleurotus cornucopiae*)

Wood Blewitt
(Lepista nuda)

Common Morel
(Morchella esculenta)

Black Morel
(Morchella elata)

Field Blewitt
(Lepista saeva)

Cep
(Boletus edulis)

Cep
(detail)

Trumpet Chanterelle
(*Cantharellus tubaeformis*)

Giant Puffball
(*Lycoperdon giganteum*)

Velvet Shank
(*Flammulina velup*

Saffron Milk Cap
(*Lactarius deliciosus*)

Saffron Milk Cap
(*detail*)

Horse Mushroom
(*Agaricus arvensis*)

Dark Cep
(Boletus aereus)

Hedgehog Mushroom
(Hydnum repandum)

Hedgehog Mushroom
(detail)

DIRECTORY OF FUNGI

AMETHYST DECEIVER *Laccaria amethystina*

A deceiver sounds as though it is a poisonous mushroom
disguised as an edible one; in fact, its common name comes
from the appearance of its fruiting bodies, which varies hugely,
so this is a mushroom that takes time to get to know. The
basic Deceiver, as opposed to the amethyst variety, is flesh
coloured, edible and very common, but it does take a little
time to learn to identify it with confidence, so the focus here
is on its tastier and brilliantly jewel-coloured relative.

DESCRIPTION: The cap is depressed in the centre, but flattens
out towards the margins as it grows, reaching between 1–6cm
(½–2½in). The Amethyst Deceiver's most distinctive feature is
its glorious violet/lilac colour, which is found on cap, gills and
stem. It fades somewhat as it matures to a pale lilac buff and
the cap and stem can appear to be dusted with white powder.
Pick it when the colour is still good – partly to aid
identification, but also because it tastes better when young.
SPORE PRINT: White.
SEASON: Through summer and autumn.
WHERE TO FIND: Woodland, both deciduous and conifer –
common in beech woods.
LOOK-ALIKES: The Lilac Fibrecap (*Inocybe geophylla var.
lilacina*) appears at the same time of year as the Amethyst
Deceiver, but must be avoided because all Fibrecaps are
poisonous. A key difference is the colour of the spore print,
which is emphatically brown; also the edge of the cap tends to
split – remember these distinctions and mistakes won't occur.
In addition, the Lilac Fibrecap smells and tastes unpleasant –

but I trust you will be careful enough not to go so far as to taste it! The violet-coloured varieties of Webcap (*Cortinarius*) should also be avoided; these have rusty-brown spore prints to distinguish them and are probably closer in appearance and more likely to be confused with a Blewits (*Lepista*).

COOKING: Clean thoroughly before cooking as the gills are closely packed and can retain dirt. I personally think this mushroom is delicious eaten fresh. The stalks are tough and not worth cooking. The cap has a slightly sweet and very delicate flavour; for more of an impact mix it with stronger-flavoured mushrooms in stews. Part of the appeal of this mushroom is its colourful beauty on the plate – mix it with egg-yolk yellow Chanterelles for stunning effect.

BEEFSTEAK FUNGUS *Fistulina hepatica*

The Beefsteak Fungus is a bracket fungus (see p.7) with a rich flavour and a dense, meaty texture – but it does require careful cooking to bring out the best and is not to everyone's taste. One of its advantages is that it is impossible to mistake it for anything else, looking as it does very much like a slice of meat and generally, but not exclusively, found lurking around the base of the tree trunk. It is a parasitic fungus and causes dark rings on the tree, resulting in attractive and much valued timber.

DESCRIPTION: The French call this fungus Ox-tongue, which is a near-perfect description. Semi-circular in shape, it can vary in size from 10–23cm (4–9in) across and a meaty 2–6cm (¾–2½in) thick; blood red in colour, with creamy pores on the underside which, somewhat spookily given its fleshy appearance, exude small drops of red fluid. When sliced it does bear an extraordinary resemblance to a piece of fat meat.

SPORE PRINT: White.

SEASON: Late summer to autumn.

Where to find: On the base of deciduous trees, usually oaks, but occasionally sweet chestnut.

LOOK-ALIKES: The Beefsteak is a distinctive fungus – nothing comes close to it.

COOKING: Best when fresh; when it is maturing it is simply not worth the bother of cooking. The bitter juice from the Beefsteak will spoil its flavour so remove the pores and the skin and always pre-cook it before adding it to any dish, to sweat out its juices. The section that is closest to the tree will be very tough and hard to eat so that should be trimmed away too. Cook it slowly and gently in butter and perhaps a little stock. It is also good in stews; fry it in a little butter first, then add it to the stew for the last half hour of cooking. It dries well; cut it into thin strips first.

FIELD BLEWITS OR BLUE LEG *Lepista saeva*

Blewits are rather unprepossessing seen from above, but very pretty from below where their subtle colouring can be appreciated. This fungus has distinctive violet to blue stems, hence its other common name of Blue Leg. It was popular in the Midlands, where it was traditionally regarded as an acceptable substitute for tripe. The Field Blewits is not very common, but where it does occur it is likely to be abundant; pick it young to avoid maggot infestations.

DESCRIPTION: The buff to grey caps are flat and irregular and curl under at the edges, they have a diameter of 5–13cm (2–5in). The flesh has a translucent, jelly-like appearance and a faintly fruity perfume. The gills are white or greyish pink and the blue to violet stems are swollen at the base.

SPORE PRINT: Pale pink.

SEASON: October to early winter.

WHERE TO FIND: In rough pastures, often in rings. Best picked in dry weather.

LOOK-ALIKES: Other woodland fungi with violet coloration on the cap, gills or stem can cause serious stomach upsets (see Look-alikes under Amethyst Deceiver). As a simple rule of thumb, if the spore print is brown or rusty brown, then the fungus is not a Blewits and should not be consumed.

COOKING: The Field Blewits has a slippery texture and a mildly spicy flesh with a robust flavour. It is often used as flavouring for soups and stews, but do try cooking it with garlic as this is a heavenly combination. When trying it for the first time only have a small portion as it can cause stomach upsets in some people. Never eat it raw: its toxicity is removed by cooking, rendering it safe to eat.

WOOD BLEWITS *Lepista nuda*

The Wood Blewits is smaller and more delicate than the Field Blewits, and the colour of its cap, gills and stalk are a more pronounced violet blue.

DESCRIPTION: The smooth, violet to tan-brown caps are convex, with wavy and irregular margins that curl under like a page-boy haircut. They have a diameter of 5–15cm (2–6in). The flesh has a bluish tinge. The gills are darker than the cap and violet or greyish pink fading to buff. The blue to violet stems are swollen at the base.

SPORE PRINT: Pale pink.

SEASON: Wood Blewits appear from late September and continue into the New Year, defying the frosts that finish off so many other mushrooms.

WHERE TO FIND: Among leaf litter in deciduous and coniferous woods. More common than the Field Blewits.

LOOK-ALIKES: Other woodland fungi with violet coloration on the cap, gills or stem can cause serious stomach upsets (see Look-alikes under Amethyst Deceiver). As a simple rule of thumb, if the spore print of the look-alike is brown or rusty brown then the fungus is not a Blewits and should not be consumed.

COOKING: The Wood Blewits has a delicious fruity flavour and smell. When trying this mushroom for the first time only have a small portion as it can cause stomach upsets in some people. Never eat it raw; its toxicity is removed by cooking, rendering it safe to eat.

GREEN CRACKED BRITTLEGILL *Russula viriscens*

A large proportion of Brittlegill species are edible, although telling one species from another can be challenging. As the name suggests most fungi in this genus have gills that are just that – brittle. Once you have seen a Brittlegill you will be confident in identifying others from the family. Though, as always there are exceptions; notably the Charcoal Burner (*Russula cyanoxantha*), which has flexible gills but is also edible. The Green Cracked Brittlegill is not found in great abundance, unlike the Common Yellow Brittlegill (*Russula ochroleuca*) which while edible in theory, has a rather peppery flavour like many of the Brittlegills. If you are fortunate enough to find one, the Green Cracked Brittlegill has a pleasant, mild flavour.

DESCRIPTION: Distinctive greenish hue, dotted with patches of sea-green, brown and ochre – not especially appealing. The skin of the cap, which starts depressed with down-turned edges, rapidly flattens out; cracks hint at the white flesh beneath. The flesh, gills and plump stem are all white, though the stem can acquire brown stains – all have a faint aroma of hazelnuts.

SPORE PRINT: White to cream.

SEASON: Summer and early autumn.

WHERE TO FIND: Broad-leaved woods, notably beech or oak.

LOOK-ALIKES: There are a number of similar fungi, the most alarming of which is the Death Cap (*Amanita phalloides*). Its cap is an olive green and the gills and spores white. Key features to note in the Death Cap are the obvious white ring on the stem and the bulbous volva at the base of the stem. There are also other green *Russulas*, some of which are edible, others can cause stomach upsets.

COOKING: Best eaten fresh. Take care to clean it carefully because maggots are also rather partial to it. Don't over cook: try it fried or grilled. It can be used raw in salads.

CEP OR PENNY BUN *Boletus edulis*

The Cep is a delicious mushroom for gourmet palates and is generally better known by its Italian name, *Porcini*. It is very popular in Europe. When you pick a Cep, break a small piece off the cap: if the flesh stays white it is a Cep; if it changes colour you have gathered a similar species – though many *Boletus* species are edible so don't automatically discount it. When you are picking a Cep, hold the stem near its base and twist to pull it up, to ensure the whole mushroom is removed. If you use any other method, such as cutting it out with a knife, you risk leaving a little flesh in the ground, which can damage the mycelium and prevent further crops.

DESCRIPTION: The Cep has a smooth, dry, polished top, that looks somewhat like a bun – or at least a children's illustration of a bun – and measures 5–30cm (2–12in) in diameter. The cap looks increasingly polished as the fungi ages. The underside is a mass of white sponge-like pores that turn yellow and finally green with age. The stem is short and squat, bulbous at the base and coloured fawn and white; it is covered with tiny markings which, close to the cap, resemble snakeskin. Also included in the *Boletus* family are the Bay Bolete and Dark Cep (see following page).

SPORE PRINT: Brown.

SEASON: August to November.

WHERE TO FIND: Woodland clearings.

LOOK-ALIKES: There are numerous species of *Boletus*, the principal edible varieties are listed below, though there are many more than there is space for here. Some varieties are inedible and one is poisonous: it has distinctive red stripes at its base and when mature the pores turn a similar red colour so it is hard to confuse with a true Cep. Essentially avoid any *Boletus* with orange or red pores.

COOKING: Some fastidious types recommend removing the pores, so that you are just left with the flesh of the cap, but this seems a terrible waste and is really only necessary if the fungi are at all soggy. It is worth checking for maggots – though young specimens are generally maggot free! The Cep is a delicious fungi that can be eaten raw in salads, but equally will enhance any number of dishes. It is wonderful simply fried in butter with plenty of salt and eaten solo or on toast. Ceps are at their best when young, but they also dry very well and are useful to have on standby.

BAY BOLETE *Boletus badius*

In my local woods in south-east Kent, the Bay Bolete abounds.
Like the Cep, it resembles a bun, but the key difference is in
the pores, which are yellow and bruise a dramatic blue on
touching. Don't worry about this exotic colour staining: it
vanishes on cooking. The Bay Bolete is delicious, with one
proviso: only pick young specimens and do so during dry
weather. After wet weather they swell to fantastic sizes and
acquire the taste and texture of an aged soggy sponge. You
don't have to pick them to establish this fact, just reach
underneath the cap and touch the pores on the underside:
if they are not firm but soft, springy or even soggy, then
leave them where they are to carry on releasing spores.
Look for them in the same places as the Cep and follow the
same instructions.

DARK CEP *Boletus aureus aereus*

The Dark Cep is another delicious mushroom, but it is much
less common than the Cep or the Bay Bolete. If you are lucky
enough to find it, enjoy the experience and utilise it as you
would the Cep. The look is still that of a bun, but, as its name
indicates, it is darker in colour, a rich brown with patches
near the edge of the cap taking on an intense brick-red hue.
The flesh is white and the pores a creamy white, but turning
yellow with age; it has a strong mushroomy perfume. The
stem is very short and stout and it is networked with tiny
markings like dots. Like the two previous Boletes, the spore
print is brown. It is found in similar locations, though is
especially partial to oak woods.

CAULIFLOWER FUNGUS *Sparassis crispa*

The Cauliflower Fungus does not fit most people's idea of a mushroom, resembling, as its name indicates, a good-sized cauliflower – though equally a brain (it is also sometimes called Brain Fungus), a piece of coral, a natural sponge or even a head of lettuce. Spotting one is a real fungi forager's find, for not only is it delicious, it has the advantage of growing to plus-size proportions, so just one can feed the whole family. Please see note on conservation on p.7.

DESCRIPTION: The Cauliflower Fungus has no obvious cap, stem or gills, instead it is a network of flat, spore-bearing branches that form a generous dome, commonly reaching an impressive 30cm (12in) across or more. The stem is buried in the soil. The flesh is white, getting tougher the closer it gets to the stalk and it smells faintly of hazelnuts.

SPORE PRINT: Creamy white to very pale yellow.

SEASON: Late summer and autumn.

WHERE TO FIND: At the base of pine trees. It will appear reliably in the same spot for many years, so once you have found one you can look forward to an annual treat. If the fungus is very large, just cut off a section and leave the rest to mature and release spores.

LOOK-ALIKES: This is a fairly unique mushroom, so it is hard to make a mistake as long as you follow the description. You might possibly confuse it with Hen-in-the-Woods (*Grifola frondosa*), which really resembles a brown flower made up of numerous overlapping lobes, with white pores on the underside – so frankly, in my opinion, you'd need to see an optician if you muddled the two. It is also found at the base of trees, but in broad-leaved woodland rather than coniferous. On the plus side, Hen-in-the-Woods is also edible, but only when young and fresh. It is somewhat tough and does best when cooked slowly over a long period of time.

COOKING: Use only young specimens. Cut away the stem and lower sections, which will be tough. Once this fungus has started to yellow with age, the whole fruiting body will be too fibrous to eat with any pleasure. Clean it carefully, for as it grows it envelops all manner of objects from the forest floor – as well as providing a home to interesting quantities of wildlife. I have eaten it deep fried in a light tempura batter – a divine mix of flavour and texture. It dries very well: cut it into smaller pieces first.

CHANTERELLE/GIROLLE *Cantharellus cibarius*

The Chanterelle is a beautiful mushroom with distinctive egg-yolk yellow flesh; on menus it often goes by its French name girolle. I once spent ten minutes hurling abuse at the TV screen because a chef on a cookery programme kept talking about Chanterelle and Girolle as two separate species. To my chagrin I later discovered that in France only *Cantharellus cibarius* is called Girolle, while the Golden Chanterelle (*C. aurora*) and the Trumpet Chanterelle (*C. tubaeformis*), detailed in a separate listing below, are referred to as Chanterelle – hence the confusion. All three are edible and in the UK all three tend to be known as plain Chanterelle. This species is so distinctive that it is supposedly hard to confuse and therefore a good starting point for would-be collectors. This is true to a point, the Chanterelle does not look like any other fungi, but, and it is a big BUT, it is quite tricky to tell a *bona fide* Chanterelle from its close relative the False Chanterelle (*Hygrophoropsis aurantiaca*).

DESCRIPTION: The cap's diameter ranges from 2–15cm (¾–6in). It has blunt ridges instead of gills, which flare upwards and outwards to the lip of the horn-shaped cap so that the centre of the cap is depressed. The stem tapers to the base and is *not* hollow, unlike some of its relatives – though if it has been attacked by insects that difference can be hard to discern. A key identification tool is its distinctive scent, rather like that of ripe plums or apricots.

SPORE PRINT: Pale yellow or white.

SEASON. June to October.

WHERE TO FIND: Mixed and coniferous woods – often found close to beech and oak, or on mossy banks. In Scotland, where they are very common, they are found in pine and birch woods This is one case where you should try to cut the stem rather than pull it; this will help the fungus regenerate and keep the supply going.

LOOK-ALIKES: The False Chanterelle (*Hygrophoropsis aurantiaca*) looks somewhat similar but, like a perma-tanned footballer's wife, it is bright orange rather than golden yellow and lacks the distinctive smell of apricots. The gills are true gills, unlike those on the Chanterelle; this is a bit of a technical point for the beginner, as even when you're looking at the two side by side it can take a moment to spot the difference. A key identification pointer can be the fact that the cap is rolled under quite distinctly on the False Chanterelle. Irritatingly it is more common than the Chanterelle. The spore print is white. The poisonous and rare Jack O'Lantern (*Omphalotus illudens*) looks very similar, though it is almost luminous and has a very unpleasant smell. The spore print is also white.

The Fool's Webcap (*Cortinarius orellanus*), found in the south east, and the Deadly Webcap (*C. rubellus*), found in Scotland, both have reddish brown caps, rusty-brown spore prints and are rare, but highly toxic. The Deadly Webcap has widely spaced gills, a stem that often carries the remnants of yellow cobwebby veil and a faint smell of radish. The Fool's Webcap's distinctive feature is that it has purplish flesh that turns red a few minutes after it has been cut or bruised.

The aforementioned Golden Chanterelle (*C. aurora*) is edible, though perhaps not boasting quite so perfect a flavour. It has an orange yellow cap with brownish hairs, a bright yellow and hollow stem, pale yellowish brown gills and a pale orange spore print. It does not have a distinctive smell.

COOKING: The Chanterelle is a gourmet mushroom prized by discerning chefs for its delectably subtle, slightly peppery flavour, combined with a superb texture. It has very dense flesh and should be chewy – take care not to overcook it or it can become tough. It can be bitter when raw so should be cooked, even if using in salads. Wonderful with omelettes or scrambled eggs and delicious fried. Chanterelles do not preserve well and are best eaten fresh, though will keep in the fridge for a few days. A fringe benefit with these fungi is that they are generally maggot free. Chanterelles are regularly on sale in open-air markets in Europe.

TRUMPET OR WINTER CHANTERELLE
Cantharellus tubaeformis

This mushroom is related to both the Chanterelle and the Horn of Plenty. It is common enough, but it is the very devil to spot, for it thrives in leaf litter and blends in with its surroundings. The good news that where you uncover one, you will probably find plenty more – so keep hunting. It is one of my personal favourites and I like it best of all cooked in butter and popped on top of a pile of creamy scrambled eggs and an English muffin.

DESCRIPTION: The cap of the Trumpet Chanterelle is browner in colour than the Chanterelle, but it has the same shape – convex, depressed in the centre, flattening out into a funnel shape as it grows, with the margins becoming wavy. It measures from 2–6cm (¾–2½in) in diameter. Its underside is covered with a network of delicate white gills that look like veins standing out against a brown relief. The yellow stem is 5–8cm (2–3in) in height and is hollow. The Trumpet Chanterelle fruits late in the season, when other supplies of mushrooms have dried up.

SPORE PRINT: Creamy to pale yellow.

SEASON: Autumn and often up to Christmas and beyond.

WHERE TO FIND: Leaf litter and moss and under conifers, especially pines.

LOOK-ALIKES: The Trumpet Chanterelle is also known as Yellow Legs and this is one of its key identification features, along with the shape of the cap: focus on these and you really can't go wrong in identifying this species.

COOKING: Cut the stem when you collect it, instead of pulling it up and bringing a mass of leaf litter with it – this saves on cleaning it. The flesh is thinner than that of the Chanterelle but it has a sweet and pleasant flavour and an aromatic perfume and, as an added bonus, it is exquisitely pretty on the plate.

CHARCOAL BURNER *Russula cyanoxantha*

In the family of Brittlegills the Charcoal Burner is an interesting deviation from the brittle rule – its gills being entirely flexible. Key to identifying this species is to be certain that all the identification points match precisely; for example, if the caps are much larger, or smaller, then you may have another species. Some *Russulas* are edible and delicious; some won't hurt you, but frankly taste less than desirable; others are downright toxic. This is a family that you must take great care with and one that takes time to learn to identify confidently.

DESCRIPTION: The colour of the cap is a curious mix of colours incorporating blue, yellow, green and purple – in theory, the colour of a charcoal burner's flame – though not many of us can verify that fact from experience. It can grow impressively large, with the diameter of the cap ranging from 5–15cm (2–6in). It starts rounded and flattens out with age. The gills are white and distinctly flexible and somewhat greasy to the touch. The stem is also white and grows from 5–10cm (2–4in). The Charcoal Burner has very little scent.

SPORE PRINT: White.

SEASON: Summer through to autumn.

WHERE TO FIND: Broadleaved woods, especially beech.

LOOK-ALIKES: *Russula langei* is very similar indeed to the Charcoal Burner, though the gills are cream instead of white and the stem often daubed with purple patches. The good news is it is also edible. Similarly *R. parazurea* is also edible, but its cap is more of a bluish grey in colour, the gills are cream and the crumbly flesh yellow. The Blackening Russula (*R. nigricans*) has a brownish black cap and gills, though the caps of young specimens are white mottled with brown and the gills are yellow. It is helpful to note that the flesh bruises a deep pinkish red when damaged. It is edible when very young, but quickly becomes infested with slugs and frankly the taste really doesn't warrant the effort of cooking. *Russula fragilis* has a purplish pink cap, it is much smaller than the Charcoal Burner and smells fruity and unpleasant. The margin of the cap has a distinctive edge like the teeth of a saw.

COOKING: Young specimens are best; older mushrooms are often infested with maggots. The flesh is thick but the flavour is very mild. Cook with garlic or lemon to give it an edge.

CHICKEN OF THE WOODS *Laetiporus sulphureus*

As its name implies, this fungus is somewhat reminiscent of chicken and you can use it as a replacement for the meat should the occasion demand. It is instantly recognisable and has no real look-alikes so would seem incredibly safe. However, a note of caution: a very few people have adverse reactions to it, suffering dizziness and nausea. Always cook it before eating and, as an extra safeguard, the first time that you try it, sample just a small amount; then if it does not agree with you, the impact is minimal. Beware of specimens growing on yew: bracket fungi digest heartwood and can absorb the toxins from the tree and become very poisonous themselves. Never, ever, pick a Chicken of the Woods that is growing on a yew tree. Please see note on conservation on p.7.

DESCRIPTION: This distinctive bracket fungus has an almost luminous sulphur-yellow colour when young. It has a smooth, undulating profile as it grows in tiers down the tree trunk. Mature specimens can grow to mighty proportions, with weights of 22kg (48lb) being recorded. The young flesh is moist and can produce drops when squeezed; the texture is distinctly chicken like.

SPORE PRINT: White.

SEASON: It appears in early summer, but the fruiting body can remain on the tree throughout winter, by which time it will be much too old and tough to eat.

WHERE TO FIND: Chicken of the Woods grows on oak, chestnut, beech and willow. Never pick specimens growing on yew (see above). There's no need to remove the whole fungus when you find it; you can merely cut out a chunk of young flesh for supper.

LOOK-ALIKES: None.

COOKING: Always cook Chicken of the Woods; never eat it raw. The first time you sample it try only a very small piece (see above). Cook only young specimens – the fungus gets tough with age – and remove the section closest to the trunk as this can contain particles of bark. Chicken of the Woods has a mild flavour and a strong fungi perfume; it can be used as any other mushroom in stews, sauces and soups, but it can also be treated as a piece of meat and grilled. It can be dried and powdered for later use in sauces and stews, but my personal health and safety rule is to only use it fresh. This ensures I don't add it to dishes without thinking and serve it to guests who may have an adverse reaction to it.

FAIRY RING CHAMPIGNON *Marasmius oreades*

Legend has it that fairies dance within the rings created by these mushrooms. The less romantic fact is that the rings are caused by the mycelium leaching nutrients from the soil. The mycelium expands outwards in search of fresh nutrients, releasing nitrogen as it goes creating an area of lush growth. This dear little mushroom is one of the culinary gems, with a superb flavour and a sweet grassy perfume. It grows just about everywhere and is easy to recognise. But don't work on the principle that any mushroom growing in a ring fits the bill – that would be a big mistake, as some are deadly poisonous. Take care to master the key identification points and you won't make a fatal error. Fungi identification courses are really helpful in learning to recognise species such as this with confidence.

DESCRIPTION: The cap and stem are a smooth tawny pinkish colour. The cap is initially shaped like a nipple-topped bell, darker in the centre, but it flattens out with age, measuring just 2–5cm (¾–2in) in diameter. The gills are a tawny cream and are widely shaped and interspersed with shorter gills near the margins of the cap, which is often grooved. The thin elastic stems grow to heights of 3–8cm (1¼–3¼in) and are a creamy colour. You can often see a clearly identifiable ring in the grass and this is helpful to note.

SPORE PRINT: White.

SEASON: Spring to autumn.

WHERE TO FIND: In any kind of short, cut grass – anywhere.

LOOK-ALIKES: The Fool's Funnel (*Clitocybe rivulosa*) and the Ivory Funnel (*C. dealbata*) both also have white spores and both are seriously toxic, so take great care that you have not confused the species. The Fool's Funnel appears from late summer to autumn and also grows in rings, but the 3–4cm (1¼–1½in) dirty white cap is generally depressed in the centre, though it can on occasion have a teat. The gills are white with pink specks. Like the Fairy Ring Champignon the flesh of the Fool's Funnel also has a grassy perfume. It is uncommon, but *never* make assumptions: if you are not sure, don't eat it. The Ivory Funnel is convex with a central depression; the cap is buff in colour, the gills white to cream and the white stem rather sturdier than that of the Fairy Ring Champignon. It has a distinctive mealy 'fragrance'.

COOKING: Discard the tough stems and check carefully for maggots as the Fairy Ring Champignon can become infested. It has a lovely flavour that enhances soups, sauces and stews to great effect. It is also delicious fried. It dries very well, quickly recovering its pretty shape when popped into water.

FIELD MUSHROOM *Agaricus campestris*

The Field Mushroom belongs to the *Agaricus* genus, which includes the cultivated mushroom *Agaricus bisporus* that we are all most familiar with from the supermarkets. Never let this fact lull you into a false sense of security, for some of our best-known poisonous specimens are also close relatives, including the Death Cap (*Amanita phalloides*) and the Destroying Angel (*A. virosa*). These alarming monikers are well deserved; the Death Cap and the Destroying Angel kill with remarkable efficiency – just half a cap is sufficient – and they are thought to be responsible for most of the fatal mushroom poisonings worldwide, with victims taking an unhappy six to sixteen days to die. The greatest caution must be exercised when hunting for Field Mushrooms. Although there are other mushrooms that are closer look-alikes, there is not much room for error if you confuse a Death Cap or Destroying Angel with a Field Mushroom. This is a mushroom you must learn to identify on guided field trips – and never pick it in the juvenile button mushroom stage, as key identification features are not visible until the fungus matures. The long list of worryingly toxic look-alikes below will hopefully serve not as a discouragement, but highlight the need for caution. There are a number of edible mushrooms that can be mistaken for the Field Mushroom, but my primary concern is highlighting the dangerous ones.

DESCRIPTION: The cap is white and smooth to the touch; there are sometimes a few brown fibres towards its centre. It starts out as a dumpy button shape, matures into a nice round cap, and eventually becomes flat, ranging in diameter from 6–10cm (2½–4in). The gills start off as a warm pink, but turn brown as the fungus matures. The white stem is a nice solid round when young, becoming spongy with age and bruising brown; it grows from 5–8cm (2–3¼in) in height. When young the mushroom will be enclosed in a veil – cut it open and you should see the pink gills – but please remember never eat it at this immature stage for safety. When the veil is broken small tattered remnants should still be visible on the stem. The flesh of the mushroom is white, but reddens minutely when it is cut.

SPORE PRINT: Dark brown.

SEASON: Summer through to autumn.

WHERE TO FIND: In short grass that is mown or grazed, often forming rings.

LOOK-ALIKES: The Yellow-staining Mushroom (*Agaricus xanthodermus*) is the species that most resembles the Field Mushroom. Although it is not as spectacularly dangerous as the Death Cap and the Destroying Angel, it can make you feel very ill indeed. Strangely, some people can eat it without suffering any ill effects, but it is not a risk worth taking. It does look alarmingly like a Field Mushroom and the Horse Mushroom (*A. arvensis*) and the Wood Mushroom (*A. silvicola*), too. However, one of the key differences is that the skin close to the margin of the cap turns yellow when bruised or rubbed. This effect is more marked when it is young, but the gills also darken as it ages to further aid identification. The stem, which also stains yellow, carries a large down-turned ring a little like a decorative drooping ruff. The gills can be white or grey with age, the flesh is white but yellows when handled. It has an unpleasant odour: imagine a mix of creosote and mouse droppings with a splash of ink.

The Red-staining Inocybe (*Inocybe patouillardii*) is also poisonous – with very unpleasant effects. After much sweating and vomiting, death can be caused by heart failure or asphyxiation. It most closely resembles a Field Mushroom when it is young: as it matures the creamy cap becomes more yellow and the shape moves from bell to flat. The gills start pink, but turn yellow and then red. The spore print is the same brown as the Field Mushroom's so is no help with identification. The stem is white with red fibres. The smell is fruity when young, becoming heavier and unpleasant with age. The White Dapperling (*Leucoagaricus leucothites*) is another troublesome blighter that bears more than a passing resemblance to the Field Mushroom. Key differences are that the gills are white, acquiring a hint of pink with age and the spore print is white to pink. Finally there is the Destroying Angel, the dreadful consequences of accidentally consuming this fungi are detailed above. It looks superficially similar to the Field Mushroom, but its gills and spore print are white. If you are picking carefully, easing fungi out of the ground with a knife rather than just carelessly tugging, you will also see the volva, which looks like a swollen white bag at the base of the stem. (For a description of the Death Cap, look under The Green Cracked Brittlegill on page 53.)

COOKING: The smell and taste of this mushroom is much stronger than that of its shop-bought cousin. It has many uses and can be eaten raw in salads or introduced to any number of dishes, but please check it carefully – it can be prone to maggots. It is best eaten fresh.

HEDGEHOG MUSHROOM *Hydnum repandum*

This mushroom has much to recommend it to the novice hunter: it is common, instantly recognisable and has no toxic look-alikes. The Hedgehog Mushroom has a beautiful texture, with a cap that feels as soft as chamois leather. Most distinctive, though, is its underside where, in place of gills, it has a mass of tiny crowded spines that you will recognise the moment you see them. It is highly prized on the Continent and collected and sold in markets. Please see p.7.

DESCRIPTION: The fleshy cap can reach an impressive 3–12cm (1¼–4¾in) in diameter and ranges in colour from a creamy off-white to yellow or even orange. It starts as a neat rounded shape, but matures unevenly, becoming lumpy and depressed in the centre. On the underside of the cap is a mass of fragile white to creamy brown spines. The stem is short and squat and paler in colour than its cap, and 3–7cm (1¼–2¾in) in height. It has a lovely mushroomy smell.

SPORE PRINT: White.

SEASON: Late summer through autumn.

WHERE TO FIND: Woodland.

LOOK-ALIKES: There is some debate over the Terracotta

Hedgehog (*Hydnum rufescens*) as to whether it is a variety of the Hedgehog Mushroom or a species in its own right. Either way it looks much the same, save its orangey brown colour and rather smaller size; it is also edible.

COOKING: This delicious fungus needs to be cooked for it is slightly bitter in its raw state. It can be used when juvenile or mature, but the spines should be cut off older specimens to help remove the bitter taste. It can be cooked in any number of ways and its dense flesh makes it suitable for long slow cooking, as well as drying for future use.

HONEY FUNGUS *Armillaria mellea*

One of the reasons for including Honey Fungus is that it is so very common that everyone should be able to find it without too much difficulty. Though, having said this, it is hugely variable. The appearance of the fruiting bodies heralds the death of a tree or a shrub – bad news for gardeners. Honey Fungus spreads via thick, black, twisted and fraying 'shoelaces' called rhizomorphs, which can run along the surface of the ground and in the bark, as well as underground, spreading to infect other trees in the area. Great care should be taken when consuming this fungus as it can cause stomach upsets. It must be cooked prior to eating and only a small amount should ever be eaten at one time in case of an adverse reaction – it is thought that some varieties are more easily digested than others. In Italy and France it is sold in local markets alongside much better known culinary fungi.

DESCRIPTION: The ochre cap starts convex, then flattens out and finally becomes centrally depressed. It has darker scales at its centre and can range in diameter from 3–12cm (1¼–4¾in). The yellow stem tapers and reddens towards its base, where it joins other stems to form a thick clump on tree stumps or tree trunks. At the neck of the stem is a distinct white to yellow ring. The gills start white, turning yellow then a spotted pinkish brown.

SPORE PRINT: Cream.

SEASON: Autumn.

WHERE TO FIND: On deciduous and coniferous tree stumps and tree trunks in gardens, parks and woods.

LOOK-ALIKES: There are three species of *Armillaria* that are difficult to tell apart; as well as *A. mellea* there is *A. ostoyae* whose stem has a ring with dark brown scales around the edge of the ruff and *A. bulbosa*, which has a stout stem and a white ring. All are edible in moderation.

COOKING: Only use young fungi with white gills and discard the stems because they are tough. Blanch in boiling water for five minutes to help remove toxins. Antonio Carluccio recommends eating it sautéed in butter with garlic. This mushroom has a very rich flavour; keep portions small to avoid tummy upsets. If you don't react to eating it, and there are more fungi in the same location, you can safely eat more next time – but always be cautious when sampling it from a new location.

HORN OF PLENTY OR TRUMPET OF DEATH *Craterellus cornucopioides*

The French call this mushroom 'trompette de la mort', which doesn't sound like a good name for an edible mushroom. Its grim moniker actually refers to its appearance – not unlike a black trumpet – and not to any toxic qualities. This is a mushroom that beginners can hunt for and enjoy with impunity – nothing else looks like it, except another very tasty edible mushroom (*Cantharellus cinereus*). It is prized for its subtle flavour, which is shown off to best advantage in delicate dishes.

DESCRIPTION: The Horn of Plenty looks like a cornucopia in shape; it has almost no stalk and the giant cap is shaped like a trumpet with a wavy margin that diminishes in size to its base, growing around 3–9cm (1¼–3½in) tall with a 4cm (1½in) diameter. The wrinkled interior ranges in tone from grey to brown and black, the exterior is more resolutely grey, often with a whitish bloom.

SPORE PRINT: White.

SEASON: Late summer through to autumn.

WHERE TO FIND: Leaf litter in deciduous woods, notably oak and beech. It blends in with its surroundings and is not common. If you are fortunate enough to find one, keep looking – there are likely to be many more.

LOOK-ALIKES: The only real look-alike, *Cantharellus cinerus* is smaller than the Horn of Plenty and the exterior surface near the trumpet carries white wrinkles. It is said to smell of plums, though I haven't yet been able to establish this for myself.

COOKING: Insects tend to lodge deep in the Horn of Plenty so take care when cleaning. Brush or wash it – though purists argue that washing diminishes the flavour. If you want to be on the safe side, cut it in half lengthwise so that you can properly scrutinise the interior. The Horn of Plenty can safely be eaten raw but it doesn't taste very good; cooking brings out its best flavour. It is often used to good visual effect by contrasting its dramatic dark colour with white meat or fish, but it is splendid cooked my favourite way – sautéed with a little butter and some parsley. This fungus dries very successfully and its flavour intensifies, making it a very useful addition to sauces and stews well beyond its season.

HORSE MUSHROOM *(Agaricus arvensis)*

This giant of a mushroom is easy enough to spot growing in
the grass in rings and one alone can give you a splendid feast.
It is a member of the *Agaricus* family and the general advice
when collecting this species is to avoid anything that stains
yellow as it can give you a tummy upset, however the Horse
Mushroom has just these characteristics – it yellows with age
and with handling, a factor that can deter many inexperienced
foragers. However its distinctive aniseed fragrance sets it apart
from its poisonous relative the Yellow-staining Mushroom.
Field trips are of great help in learning to identify this
delicious and common fungus with confidence.

DESCRIPTION: This is an impressively statuesque mushroom
which can measure anything from 5–15cm (2–6in) in height
with a cap which can spread from 5–20cm (2–8in). The cap
starts smooth and rounded, flattening out with age. It is white
when young but yellows with age. The stem is sturdy and
swollen and bulbous at the base and hollows with age. It
bruises yellow, but does not yellow when cut. The gills start a
pale greyish cream and darken through pink to brown, they
are enclosed in a veil in the button stage which matures to a
large and distinctive ring on the stem with a cogwheel pattern
clearly visible on the underneath.

SPORE PRINT: Dark brown.

SEASON: It can appear in June and throughout the summer,
but is most abundant in September and October.

WHERE TO FIND: Lawns, grass verges, parks and pastures are
all good bets.

LOOK-ALIKES: The Yellow-staining Mushroom (*Agaricus
xanthodermus*) bears a close resemblance to the Horse
Mushroom; however key differences are that the cap and stem

of these poisonous fungi turn yellow when cut and it has a distinctive, musty, inky smell. Unfortunately it also grows in pastures and at the same time of year, so if you are in any doubt do not consume. The Macro Mushroom (*Agaricus urinascens*) also closely resembles the Horse Mushroom, indeed may often be confused for it, but as it is also edible – indeed delicious – this is not a problem. Its young gills are pink and the stem blushes faintly pink when cut, it has woolly scales on its stem toward the base. It also smells strongly of aniseed when young, but smells of ammonia with age, though this undesirable fragrance disappears with cooking.

COOKING: It is the young, sweet caps that are the true delicacy with a nutty flavour and a faint aniseed perfume; the stems are rather tough and generally not utilised and mature caps can taste rather bitter so are best avoided. The Horse Mushroom has a fuller flavour than its close relative the Field Mushroom. The simplest cooking method is to whack some butter in the cap, sprinkle it with salt and pepper and pop it under the grill, perhaps finished off with a sprinkling off fresh parsley – absolutely delicious. The Horse Mushroom is also fabulous fried as part of mega-breakfast of sausage, bacon and egg. The downside is that these fungi can become infested with maggots, so check carefully before shoving under the grill or you may get more protein than you bargained for.

JELLY/JUDAS'/JEW'S EAR *Auricularia auricula-judae*

A relative of the Jelly Ear is cultivated by the Chinese and is available in specialist delicatessens in the UK, but you can easily find its close relative growing in the wild. This is a very distinctive mushroom – it really is remarkably ear shaped. Its gelatinous flesh is entirely different in texture from the consistency we normally associate with fungi. Its alternative common names, above, have provoked much controversy and are said to spring from the tale that Judas Iscariot, a Jew, hung himself on an elder tree: folklore has it that the fungi 'ears' growing on the tree are a reminder of Judas' spirit. The species has acquired some 12 common names. It is really quite abundant and easy to identify but, if truth be told, I have rarely cooked the Jelly Ear, despite my best intentions to rustle up something more exotic than my traditional classic mushroom soup.

DESCRIPTION: The immature Jelly Ear looks like a fleshy pink, upside-down pudding bowl, its resemblance to an ear becomes more marked as it matures and the colour deepens to tan. The inner 'ear' is smooth; the outer surface has minute hairs.

SPORE PRINT: White.

SEASON: All year round.

WHERE TO FIND: On both living and, more commonly, dead wood, especially elder and elm.

LOOK-ALIKES: It is stretching the point slightly to include the Vinegar Cup (*Helvella acetabulum*), the Bay Cup (*Peziza badia*), and other members of the *Peziza* family under look-alikes, because they don't really. However, most are inedible, and the odd species is toxic – so don't make a careless mistake. *Peziza* have brittle flesh instead of jelly-like flesh. The Vinegar Cup does look much more like a cup than an ear.

COOKING: This is one fungus that I do not advocate sautéing with a little butter and parsley. The Jelly Ear requires a good wash, followed by long, slow cooking in liquid to render it tender enough to enjoy. It works best in Japanese and Chinese dishes, notably soups.

MOREL *Morchella esculenta*

This is a prized culinary mushroom and is doubly welcome as it fruits in spring when there are fewer fungi to collect. It is one of the best-known wild mushrooms, next to the Truffle – though blessedly much easier to stumble across. It has a wonderful flavour cooked solo but seems to combine beautifully with any number of other dishes: omelettes, risottos, soups and stews. Morels should not be eaten raw and don't eat older specimens. I whooped with delight when I found my first Morel – a strange unusually ghostly sculpture with a most disturbing fragrance. The fact that it did not precisely resemble a Morel, being all white, and that I found it in autumn rather than spring finally led me to the conclusion that my first 'Morel' was in fact a phallic Stinkhorn. The disappointment was crushing, but this is how you learn! I still whoop with delight when I come across a true Morel.

DESCRIPTION: The Morel doesn't look like a typical mushroom, but a strange, wayward sculpture. The cap resembles a brown sponge or honeycomb pitted with deep depressions; it has a short stout white stem. The cap is conical and has a diameter of 7.5–15cm (3–6in). The colour can vary from pale yellow to nearly black. It does not have gills or pores; the spores are formed in sacks called asci, which are distributed in a fine mist.

SPORE PRINT: Cream to yellow.

SEASON: April and May, often shooting up after rain, but usually only around for a few days.

WHERE TO FIND: Near trees and hedgerows and wasteland, often on ground that has been burnt. Increasingly common in gardens and car parks, where they grow on weed-suppressing bark mulches.

LOOK-ALIKES: There is only one toxic fungi that resembles the Morel and also appears in the spring; the False Morel (*Gyromitra esculenta*). A key difference between the two is that the stem of the false morel is multi chambered, like its cap – the stem of the true morel is not. In addition the cap of the False Morel is larger and does not have the honeycomb or sponge-like construction, resembling instead a lumpen, yellowish or brownish brain or screwed up piece of fabric. It is extremely toxic to some people and can kill.

COOKING: Morels should only be picked when they are firm and young. They must be cleaned thoroughly: some people recommend using a fine brush; others boil them in water for a few minutes to get rid of dead insects or grit. Whichever method you favour, cut them in half first to make the job easier. Morels dry successfully: again, cut them in half to aid effective drying. To avoid stomach upsets, do not eat this mushroom raw, or even lightly cooked. The Morel dries beautifully and is a useful addition to the store cupboard.

OYSTER MUSHROOM *Pleurotus ostreatus*

The Oyster Mushroom is now cultivated and sold fresh in many supermarkets, but the taste really does not compare to those that are found in the wild. The resemblance between the Oyster Mushroom and an oyster shell is fairly superficial; nevertheless, any aids to identification are always a good idea – just don't take them too literally.

DESCRIPTION: The Oyster Mushroom has a very short stem

and grows in tiers on tree trunks. The shape of the smooth, moist cap can be loosely defined as resembling an oyster shell; its wavy margins curl towards the gills. Its colour is variable, ranging from bluish grey when young to buff and white as it matures. The cap can reach from 5–15cm (2–6in) in diameter. From the underside, where the white gills radiate outwards from the stem, it more closely resembles a shell. The tough stem is woolly and white at the base though it can be absent altogether.

SPORE PRINT: Lavender.

SEASON: Most abundant in winter but can be found all year round.

WHERE TO FIND: On deciduous tree trunks, logs and tree stumps. Look upwards as well as down, when hunting for this fungus.

LOOK-ALIKES: The Pale Oyster (*Pleurotus pulmonarius*) is much the same as the Oyster Mushroom but, as its name indicates, is paler in colour; it seems to have no stem at all and its spore print is white. It is also edible, and is a popular cultivated species. The Branching Oyster (*P. cornucopiae*), also very tasty, has a more distinct and curved stem than its relatives; the cap is cream and when young covered in a white bloom; the spore print is pale lavender. It is most commonly found on dead wood and tree stumps, with elm a particular favourite. Both the Branching Oyster and the Pale Oyster have a curious floury smell, quite different to the mushroomy fragrance of the Oyster Mushroom. There are other fungi that carry this shape and some can cause stomach upsets, but none really looks like the Oyster Mushroom. If the colours do not match, if the flesh is gelatinous or slimy, then it is not a true specimen.

COOKING: The smallest Oyster Mushrooms are the tastiest; mature specimens toughen with age. Cut off the stem and discard it. The gills provide shelter to all manner of insects; give the mushrooms a good shake, then brush them carefully and wipe with a cloth. The Oyster Mushroom is delicate and doesn't keep for long, nor does it dry. The flavour is subtle; it works wonderfully well in stir fries and clear soups or cooked in a creamy sauce.

PARASOL MUSHROOM *Macrolepiota procera*

The Parasol Mushroom is delicious, common and distinctive – as long as you take care not to confuse it with a less user-friendly relative (see below). It has a characteristic and highly individual sweet fragrance but it is its whopping size that really marks it out; a Parasol cap should never be less than 8cm (3¼in) in diameter – so if you allow a good few more centimetres as a health and safety precaution, you can't go wrong.

DESCRIPTION: The cream cap commonly ranges in size from 10–25cm (4–10in) in diameter and starts small and egg shaped at the top – the Italians maintain it looks like a drumstick. It flattens as it grows, reaching giant proportions. The cap is covered with grey-brown scales in concentric rings. The gills are white, but cannot be seen until the cap opens. The stem is slender in comparison, but bulbous at its base. It has a distinctive double ring, white on top and brown below, which can be moved up and down the stem like an outsize washer. Below the ring the stem has brown markings like a snakeskin and can reach heights of 30cm (1ft). The flesh is white.

SPORE PRINT: White.

SEASON: Summer and autumn.

WHERE TO FIND: Meadows, parks, open woodland and verges.

LOOK-ALIKES: The closest look-alike is the Shaggy Parasol (*Macrolepiota rhacodes*), that is eaten and enjoyed with impunity by some people, but – and it is a big but – if you are one of the unlucky ones it can give you an upset stomach. The Shaggy Parasol looks very like the Parasol Mushroom and also has a double ring, but the cap only achieves a diameter of between 5–15cm (2–6cm). When the stem is cut it immediately blushes red and the gills bruise red, defining characteristics that make it easy to separate from its relative. It favours conifer woods. The Parasol Mushroom is also related to the Dapperlings (*Lepiota*), some of which can cause thoroughly unpleasant side effects and have colourful common names such as Death Dapperling or Stinking Dapperling. Some are edible, but the species are disconcertingly similar, so stick to the Parasol Mushroom as its size marks it out.

COOKING: Start by discarding the stalk, which is tough and inedible. Clean the cap by brushing it gently to remove dirt; the gills are quite deep so take a little time over this, but it doesn't attract many insects so it shouldn't be too problematic – washing dilutes its flavour. This mushroom has a sweet nutty taste and a texture reminiscent of chicken – it is often cooked as a huge chunk of flesh, dipped in batter and fried, or stuffed. Despite Shirley Conran maintaining in her 1970s book *Superwoman* that 'life is too short to stuff a mushroom', this is a very tasty dish and not at all complicated to make. I love the Parasol Mushroom sautéed with butter and served up with scrambled eggs for breakfast.

GIANT PUFFBALL *Calvatia gigantea*

This is one of the more astonishing fungi: a mighty mushroom, virtually the size of a football, suddenly appears in a field or on the edge of a wood, apparently overnight. Just one of these impressive fungi can serve a number of people since every bit is edible. The only important thing to check is that the flesh is white when you cut into it; if the flesh is yellowing or grey, it is not worth eating. Old Giant Puffballs will cause tummy upsets – but let's be realistic here, we don't eat a steak when it has turned green and smelly, so I am confident that anyone with an iota of common sense would not cook a Puffball that was clearly past its best-by date.

DESCRIPTION: A white sphere that can measure anything from 10–30cm (4–12in). When young the flesh is white throughout when cut; it becomes yellow and brown with age when it is ready to spore.

SPORE PRINT: The spores of the Giant Puffball are brown but a spore print can't be taken in the conventional way as the fungus splits open when mature, releasing its spores.

SEASON: July to November.

WHERE TO FIND: In meadows, gardens, under hedges and on the edges of woodland.

LOOK-ALIKES: No other Puffballs come close in size or appearance. Although Giant Puffballs are best eaten young, take care to allow them to develop sufficiently in size so that you can be sure they are indeed Giants. The appropriately named Destroying Angel (*Amanita virosa*) resembles a very young puffball in its juvenile state. A simple test is to cut the mushroom open: if you find a perfect baby mushroom encased within the outer skin you have a Destroying Angel; cutting open a Puffball will just reveal the flesh.

COOKING: Remove the thick skin, the flesh is the delicious bit. It is very good cut into steaks and fried with a little garlic and olive oil, and extra delicious if dipped first in beaten egg and then breadcrumbs. Antonio Carluccio recommends frying it in olive oil with some garlic, chopped parsley and thyme, and lemon juice. It is also good grilled or steamed, but becomes a little soggy in casseroles. The Giant Puffball can't be preserved for future use – so enjoy it fresh!

SAFFRON MILK CAP *Lactarius deliciosus*

The Saffron Milk Cap is a vividly colourful example of a fungus that, at first glance, you might be tempted to discount. It stains green so readily when bruised and the flesh exudes a milky latex that turns bright orange on contact with the air – neither of which sell it as a gastronomic treat. However its Latin name *deliciosus* reveals its true value to the hunter. It is highly prized in many countries, including France, not only for its flavour, but also for its visual impact. The flavour improves on cooking; when raw, it has a hint of bitterness. All the Milk Caps exude droplets of milk or latex: the colour of this substance is crucial to the successful identification of the different species.

DESCRIPTION: The cap of this species can reach giant proportions, ranging from 5–20cm (2–8in) in diameter. It is orange-red and turns green when damaged. The cap is convex

in the centre and becomes a shallow funnel shape as it
matures and the margins point further and further upwards.
It features red dotted concentric rings. The surface becomes
slimy when wet. The crowded gills are orange, staining green.
The hollow stem is quite thick, up to 7cm (2¾in) in diameter;
it is paler than the cap but features carrot-coloured indented
freckles at the base of the stem. The flesh of the Saffron Milk
Cap is a cream yellow, it gives off a milky latex and has a
fruity smell.

SPORE PRINT: Pinky cream.

SEASON: Autumn.

WHERE TO FIND: Under conifers, especially pine. If you find
one, the chances are you will find masses.

LOOK-ALIKES: There are two species to steer well clear of. The
Woolly Milk Cap (*Lactarius torminosus*) is one of the nastiest,
at least in taste terms; it is consumed in some countries but
requires careful cooking in repeated changes of water to
remove the bitter-flavoured toxins – an unnecessary risk when
there are so many safe and delicious mushrooms around at the
same time of year. It is not dissimilar in shape to the Saffron
Milk Cap, but is more of a livid fleshy pink colour than
orange and its cap is positively shaggy, producing a feathery
effect at the margin. It exudes a white, bitter-flavoured latex
and has a creamy yellow spore print. Furthermore, it doesn't
grow under conifers but favours birch. If you are familiar with
the smell of fenugreek, you'll recognise the Woolly Milk Cap's
distinctive fragrance.

The similarly perfumed and toxic Fenugreek Milk Cap
(*Lactarius helvus*) on the other hand is found under both pine
and birch, but its brown cap and stem do not carry concentric
rings and the latex is like water. The spore print is a pinkish white.
The False Saffron Milk Cap (*L. deterrimus*) is very similar to its

namesake, the principal difference being that it turns green all over more readily and is more yellow than red in colour. The good news is that it is also edible, so a mistake won't hurt, but it is not as tasty. *Lactarius salmonicolor* has an orange to pink cap devoid of concentric rings or any hint of green. The gills and spore print are both pinky beige. It is only found near fir trees (*Abies*). This species has the most bitter, unpleasant taste and an unpleasantly fruity fragrance, but is not toxic.

COOKING: Clean the mushrooms and check the cap and hollow stem carefully; older specimens can house maggots. Rinse them and pop them in a pan of boiling water to blanch for no more than three minutes to remove any bitterness. Use them in salads, or cook them further – fried or as an ingredient in all manner of sauces.

SHAGGY INKCAP OR LAWYER'S WIG
Coprinus comatus

The Shaggy Inkcap is a hugely underrated mushroom with a very delicate flavour and fragile texture that I adore. A bonus is that it pops up in new places all over the country, often where ground has been disturbed, so it can suddenly appear where it has never been previously seen – on roundabouts, grass verges, parks and gardens. It is one edible fungus that you don't need to make a special trip to the woods or the countryside to find. The Shaggy Inkcap is very easy to identify, though one of the key ways of identifying it often means you spot it when it is too late to pick. This happens when the beautiful fungus dissolves into a black gooey mess as if by magic. The technical term for this is deliquescence and it is the means by which the spores are distributed as they ripen. If you spot some Shaggy Inkcaps in good condition pick them immediately; they come and go very quickly and you might have to wait another year to find a fresh crop.

DESCRIPTION: The Shaggy Inkcap looks like a fat finger pointing out of the grass, and it grows in dense clumps. The cap has a beige top and below this beige and white shaggy scales appear. When young the stem cannot be seen as the cap encases it, but as the fungus ages, it opens up into a fraying umbrella shape that drips black inky, slimy deposits on its surroundings. It is much taller than it is wide, growing from 10–20cm (4–8in) in height, while the cap only ranges from 3–7cm (1¼–2¾in) in diameter. The base of the cap and the gills begin white, turning pink and finally black with age. When you pick it in its youthful stage the cap tends to pull away, leaving the stem intact in the grass.

SPORE PRINT: Dark brown to black.

SEASON: Late summer to autumn.

WHERE TO FIND: In grass – in parks, verges and gardens.

LOOK-ALIKES: While this mushroom is fairly distinctive in appearance, take care not to confuse it with the Common Inkcap (*Coprinus atramentarius*). If you consume a Common Inkcap within 48 hours of drinking alcohol the consequences can be severe – vomiting and diarrhoea, palpitations and chest pains. It was once given to alcoholics to help induce 'a cure'; teetotallers can eat it with impunity. My personal preference is to have a glass of wine and steer clear of the Common Inkcap altogether. It is much dumpier than the Shaggy Inkcap; the cap is shorter, greyer and more bulbous, reaching just 3–7cm (1¼–2¾in) in length. It appears from spring through to late autumn and has a brown spore print. It is often found growing on wood that has been buried in grass. It was once commonly used to produce ink, by boiling mature specimens in water. The Magpie Inkcap (*C. picaceus*) looks the same as the Shaggy Inkcap when young, though a little shorter as the cap only grows to 5–8cm (2–3in) tall. As it matures it turns brown and then black with white patches – hence its common name. It smells unpleasant, which is a helpful identifier. The spores are black. It appears from late summer to autumn and favours beech woods. It can cause a toxic reaction if eaten.

COOKING: This is a mushroom that must be eaten young, when the flesh is white and there is no hint of any inkiness. It's not that the ink is poisonous; it just doesn't make for a pleasant culinary experience. So if you spot a group of Shaggy Inkcaps dissolving into a sea of black slime do not despair, keep your eyes peeled and you may well spot another clump emerging nearby a day or so later, enabling you to pick them at their peak. This mushroom is said to be sublime when dipped in tempura and fried, but I never seem to have the time: I simply adore Shaggy Inkcaps fried in butter with a little parsley and salt – total perfection.

St George's Mushroom *Calocybe gambosa*

The beauty of this common mushroom is that, as its name suggests, it tends to first appear around St George's Day, 23 April – a helpful identifier. It is freely available throughout May, but rarely seen by June. It tastes best when young, as, rather like the rest of us it toughens with age. It is much sought after by the French and Italians who appreciate its distinctive taste. Take care to identify it correctly, as it can be confused with poisonous species.

DESCRIPTION: The St George's Mushroom has a domed cap when young, which flattens with age and the margin becomes wavy. It can be white or a creamy buff in colour and has a diameter of 5–15cm (2–6in). The stem, which has no ring, and the gills are both white. The St George's Mushroom has a distinctive smell, commonly described as 'mealy', which can be off-putting when picking it, but it disappears on cooking.

SPORE PRINT: White.

SEASON: April to June.

WHERE TO FIND: On chalky soil, most common on grassland, lawns, pastures and roadsides, although you may come across them on woodland borders. It grows in rings, so if you find one, more may well be close by.

LOOK-ALIKES: It can be confused with the Deadly Fibrecap (*Incoybe erubescens*), which justly deserves its alarming name – it is extremely toxic. It also forms in rings and has a creamy white cap, but the gills are buff and the spore print is brown – so if in any doubt, a spore print will clarify identification. The Deadly Fibrecap makes its appearance rather later in the year in the summer months, another useful pointer. The Red-staining Inocybe (*Incoybe patouillardii*), is also somewhat similar in appearance and toxic, but it has reddish fibres on the cap and pink to brown gills. The stems and flesh bruise red and the sport print is brown.

COOKING: Best collected young when the flesh is firm. There is some debate about the culinary worth of this mushroom: Jane Grigson was decidedly not a fan, but Antonio Carluccio appreciates its delicate flavour. It is delicious when cooked simply with a little butter and perhaps some garlic and cream.

SUMMER TRUFFLE *Tuber aestivum*

If you thought that the gourmet Truffle was only found on the continent then think again. The Summer Truffle is a delicacy found in the UK; it is rare, but within certain areas can be locally common. It may even be more prolific than we think: the problem is finding it, as it grows underground.

DESCRIPTION: The Summer Truffle is basically a misshapen, lumpen, mass, measuring 3–7cm (1¼–2¾in) in diameter. It is brownish black in colour and covered with warty lumps – attractive! The flesh is white when young, turning a brownish grey with age and it has a strong perfume.

SPORE PRINT: Not possible to make one. The spores are distributed by animals. They are attracted to the smell of the fungus, which they eat, then the spores are distributed via their droppings.

SEASON: Summer to early winter, but specimens are sometimes found in late winter.

WHERE TO FIND: In woodland, most commonly beech, growing in chalky soil. Truffles do not appreciate ground cover above them and discourage it by depriving the soil of nutrients; so start hunting among bare patches of ground, just a few centimetres below the surface. If you are lucky, the Truffle will just be breaking the surface of the soil. Great care should be taken when searching; it is irresponsible to dig up large areas of woodland. The simplest method is to train a dog with the aid of a little Truffle oil. Breeds that use their nose for hunting are generally up to the task; my sight hounds are of no use whatsoever. The training process is not complicated and the dog can pick up the scent from 50m (164ft). The flavour of the Truffle intensifies as it matures in the ground.

LOOK-ALIKES: There are other species of Truffle in the UK;

some look like burnt cookies, others like potatoes and they range in colour from black through amber, beige and yellow. They are all edible, but remember that being edible does not necessarily make them desirable to eat.

COOKING: The Summer Truffle does not have the gastronomic kudos of the White Truffle (*Tuber magnatum*) or the Périgord or Black Truffle (*Tuber melanosporum*). Take care when handling and storing Truffles as the aroma permeates everything. Don't keep them for long once they have been dug as they quickly deteriorate. Antonio Carluccio advocates cleaning them with a fine wire brush – the type used to clean suede shoes. The taste of the Summer Truffle is distinctly nutty: it can be eaten raw, shaved over risotto, pasta and salads; added to a duck liver pâté to give an extra special flavour; or cooked in sauces and stuffing.

VELVET SHANK *Flammulina velutipes*

This common mushroom must have been even more abundant with the tragic advent of Dutch Elm Disease in the 1970s, which decimated the countryside, but allowed the Velvet Shank to proliferate on its favourite species of dead wood – the elm. The Velvet Shank has a gentle flavour that is not to everyone's taste, but it is unusual in fruiting copiously in winter when little else is around, so mushroom hunters treasure it. In Japan a cultivated variety called *enoki* is popular.

DESCRIPTION: The yellow caps of the Velvet Shank range in size from just 2–10cm (¾–4in). They change in colour as they mature from yellow to orange and the colour fades at the edge of the cap. The texture is somewhat slippery, even slimy when wet, but matt when dry. The broad gills are yellow to tan. The brown curving stems, the distinguishing feature of the species, are conspicuously tufted and velvety, fading towards the cap to a yellow tone. The mushrooms grow in tiered groups and have a sweet, but musty smell.

SPORE PRINT: White.

SEASON: Can be found all year but most abundant in winter and surviving frost and snow.

WHERE TO FIND: On dead wood, notably that of elm, beech and poplar.

LOOK-ALIKES: Beware the Sulphur Tuft (*Hypholoma fasciculare*), which also grows on dead wood and is found year round. The key difference in identification is that the Sulphur Tuft does not have a velvety stem and the stem has a faint mark where the ring has been. The gills are yellow when young, but turn a greenish brown with age, while the spore print is purple. The Sulphur Tuft tastes very bitter, so if you cook what you think is a Velvet Shank and it tastes vile then spit it out – the toxins are very nasty and cause few symptoms while they are damaging the liver. The aptly named Funeral Bell (*Galerina marginata*) is unfortunately another one to look out for. Eating this fungus can be fatal. It appears in autumn, but can still be seen in winter if the weather is mild. It differs from the Velvet Shank in that the stem has a fleshy ring, it smells unpleasant and it has a rusty brown spore print. Unlike the Velvet Shank, it doesn't have a velvety, dark brown stem, so it isn't that similar – but caution should be the watchword when any species is so very toxic. If in doubt take a spore print and you won't go wrong.

COOKING: Store Velvet Shanks in the refrigerator in a plastic bag, but don't keep them for long as their already subtle flavour gradually diminishes. Discard the tough stems, wipe the caps, or, if you prefer, peel them to remove any stickiness. The flavour is pleasant but subtle: adding a few stronger flavoured mushrooms pumps up the impact no end, but at this time of year when there is so little alternative around they are much appreciated. As with the Shaggy Inkcap, the Velvet Shank is delicious fried in a little butter and parsley. They are very pretty in soups and stews and feature in many Asian dishes.

USEFUL
ORGANISATIONS

ASSOCIATION OF BRITISH FUNGUS GROUPS
Harveys
Alston
Axminster
Devon EX13 7LG
www.abfg.org
The UK's leading voluntary fungus conservation body. ABFG members are all amateur enthusiasts and there are local groups across the country.

BRITISH MYCOLOGICAL SOCIETY
City View House
Union Street
Manchester M12 4JD
www.britmycolsoc.org.uk
The sole objective of the BMS is to promote mycology in all its aspects. It holds meetings, issues publications and runs workshops and forays for field mycologists.

COUNTRYSIDE COUNCIL FOR WALES ENQUIRY SERVICE
Maes y Ffynnon
Penrhosgarnedd
Bangor
Gwynedd LL57 2DW
www.ccw.gov.uk
The CCW advises the government on sustaining natural beauty, wildlife and the opportunity for outdoor enjoyment in Wales and its inshore waters.

DEPARTMENT FOR ENVIRONMENT, FOOD AND RURAL AFFAIRS (DEFRA)
Nobel House
17 Smith Square
London SW1P 3JR
www.defra.gov.uk
UK government department responsible for issues relating to the environment, food and rural affairs.

FIELD STUDIES COUNCIL
Montford Bridge
Preston Montford
Shrewsbury
Shropshire SY4 1HW
www.field-studies-council.org
The FSC is an environmental education charity committed to helping people to understand and be inspired by the natural world.

NATURAL ENGLAND
1 East Parade
Sheffield S1 2ET
www.naturalengland.org.uk
Natural England has been formed by bringing together English Nature, the landscape, access and recreation aspects of the Countryside Agency and the environmental land management functions of the Rural Development Service. The Countryside Code can be found on www.countryside.gov.uk

FORESTRY COMMISSION SCOTLAND
Forest Enterprise Scotland
1 Highlander Way
Inverness Business Park
Inverness IV2 7GB

FORESTRY COMMISSION WALES
Welsh Assembly Government
Rhodfa Padarn
Llanbadarn Fawr
Aberystwyth
Ceredigion SY23 3UR

FOREST ENTERPRISE ENGLAND
620 Bristol Business Park
Coldharbour Lane
Bristol BS16 1EJ
www.forestry.gov.uk
Government department for the protection and expansion of Britain's woodlands and forests.

THE NATIONAL TRUST
Heelis
Kemble Drive
Swindon
Wiltshire SN2 2NA
www.nationaltrust.org.uk
The National Trust is a charity committed to preserving and opening to the public many historic houses and gardens. It also manages thousands of acres of forests, fens, woods, beaches, downs and nature reserves.

SCOTTISH NATIONAL HERITAGE
Great Glen House
Leachkin Road
Inverness IV3 8NW
www.snh.gov.uk
www.outdooraccess-scotland.com

SNH works to help people to enjoy and value their natural heritage and to use it sustainably.

THE WILDLIFE TRUSTS
The Kiln
Waterside
Mather Road
Newark
Nottinghamshire NG24 1WT
www.wildlifetrusts.org
The Wildlife Trusts is a voluntary organisation dedicated to conserving the full range of the UK's habitat and species.

THE WOODLAND TRUST
Autumn Park
Dysart Road
Grantham
Lincolnshire NG31 6LL
www.woodland-trust.org.uk
The Woodland Trust is the UK's leading conservation charity dedicated solely to the protection of our native woodland heritage.

BIBLIOGRAPHY

A Passion For Mushrooms, Antonio Carluccio, Pavilion Books, 1989

Britain's Wild Larder: Fungi, Claire Lowenfeld, Faber & Faber, 1956

Collins Complete Guide to British Mushrooms & Toadstools, Paul Sterry and Barry Hughes, Collins, 2009

Complete Mushroom Book, Antonio Carluccio, Quadrille, 2003

Edible and Poisonous Fungi, Bulletin No. 23 of the Ministry of Agriculture & Fisheries, His Majesty's Stationery Office, 1945

Edible Mushrooms and Other Fungi, Michael Jordan, Blandford, 1995

Field Guide to Edible Mushrooms of Britain and Europe, Peter Jordan, New Holland Publishers (UK) Ltd, 2006

Food from the Wild, Ian Burrows, New Holland Publishers (UK) Ltd, 2005

Fungi, Shelley Evans and Geoffrey Kibby, Dorling Kindersley, 2004

Fungi, Brian Spooner and Peter Roberts, Collins, 2005

Fungi, Roy Watling, The Natural History Museum, 2003

How to Identify Edible Mushrooms, Patrick Harding, Tony Lyon, Gill Tomblin, Collins, 1996

Identifying Mushrooms, David Pegler and Brian Spooner, The Apple Press, 1994

Mushroom Feasts, Steven Wheeler, Southwater, 1999

Mushroom Magic, Michael Jordan, Elm Tree Books, 1989

Mushroom Picker's Foolproof Field Guide, Peter Jordan, Southwater, 2007

Mushroom, Johnny Acton and Nick Sandler, Kyle Cathie Ltd, 2007

Mushrooms and other Fungi: an Illustrated Guide, August Rinaldi and Vassili Tyndalo, Hamlyn, 1972

Mushrooms and Other Fungi of Great Britain and Europe, Roger Phillips, Pan Books, 1981

Mushrooms and Toadstools, Geoffrey Kibby, Oxford University Press, 1979

Mushrooms, Jacque Malouf, Conran Octopus, 2004

Mushrooms, Roger Phillips, Macmillan, 2006

Outlines of British Fungology, Rev. M.J, Berkeley, Lovell Reeve, 1860

The Encyclopaedia of Fungi of Britain and Europe, Michael Jordan, Frances Lincoln, 2004

The Mushroom Feast, Jane Grigson, Michael Joseph, 1975

INDEX

Agaricus 9, 20
A. arvensis 9, 67, 72–74
A. bisporus 10
A. campestris 9,
    66–69
A. silvicola 67
A. urinascens 74
A. xanthodermus 9, 67,
    73
Alpha amanitin 21
Amanita 19, 20, 21, 24
A. phalloides 20, 54, 66
A. virosa 21, 66, 81
Amethyst Deceiver
    49–59
Armillaria bulbosa 71
A. mellea 70–71
A. ostoyae 17, 71
Ascomycetes 20
Association of British
    Fungus Groups
    7, 14, 92
Auricularia auricula-
    judae 74–75

Basidiomycetes 20
Bay Bolete 56
Bay Cup 80–82

Cap 25, 26
Cantharellus aurora 60
C. cibarius 58–60
C. tubarformis 61–62
Cauliflower Fungus 33,
    57-58
Cep 27, 54–55, 56
Chanterelle 33, 58–60
Charcoal Burner 53,
    62–63

Chicken and mushroom
    pie 39
Chicken Of The Woods
    63
Clitocybe dealbata
    71–72
Countryside Code 6

Dapperlings 80
Dark Cep 56
Deadly Fibrecap 87
Deadly Web Cap 13, 60
Death Cap 20, 54, 66
Destroying Angel 21,
    66, 81
Drying mushrooms 32
Duxelles 43

Epping Forest 7
Evans, Nicholas 13

Fairy Ring Champignon
    17, 33, 64–66
False Chanterelle Gills
    24, 27
Girolle 58–60
Golden Chanterelle 60
Green Cracked
    Brittlegill 53–54
Grifola frondosa 57
Gyromitra esculenta 77
Gyromitrin 21

Hedgehog Mushroom
    27, 69–70
Helvella acetabulum 75
Hen-in-the-Woods 57
Herb Mushrooms 38
Honey Fungus 17,
    70–71

Honey Mushroom 17,
    18
Horn of Plenty 33,
    71–72
Horse Mushroom 67,
    72–74
Hydnum repandum
    69–70
H. rufescens 69
Hygrophoropsis
    aurantiaca 59
Hyphae 16, 17
Hypholoma fasiculare 90

Identification 24
Inocybe erubescens 87
I. geophylla var. lilacina
    49
I. patouillardii 68, 87
Ivory Funnel 65

Jack O'Lantern 60
Jelly Fungus 20
Jelly/Judas'/Jew's Ear 33,
    74–75

Laccaria amethystina
    49–50
Lactarius deliciosus
    82–84
L. deterrimus 83
L. helvus 83
L. salmonicolor 83
L. torminosus 83
Laetiporus sulphureus 63
Lawyer's Wig 84–86
Lepista 50
Lepiota 80
L. nuda 52–53
L. saeva 51–52

Leucoagaricus leucothites 68
Lilac Fibrecap 49

Macro Mushroom 73
Macrolepiota procera 79-80
M. rhacodes 79
Maggots 24
Magpie Inkcap 85
Marasmius oreades 64-66
Morchella esculenta 75-77
Morel 22, 23, 75-77
Muscarine 21
Mushroom and garlic risotto 36
Mushroom choux buns 46
Mushroom ragout on brioche 37
Mushroom soup 34
Mushroom stroganoff 40
Mushroom tart 42
Mushrooms on toast Deluxe 35
Mycelium 16, 17, 24
Mycorrhizal fungi 17

Omphalotus illudens 60
Orellanine 13, 21
Oyster Mushroom 77-79

Pale Oyster 78
Parasitic fungi 17
Parasol Mushroom 79-80
Pasta mess 47
Penny Bun 33, 54-55
Perfume 29
Peziza badia 75
Pleurotus cornucopiae 78

P. ostreatus 77-79
P. pulmonarius 78
Polly's Beef Wellington 44
Porcini 33
Pores 24
Potted Mushrooms 41

Red-staining Inocybe 68, 87
Russula cyanoxantha 53, 62-63
R. fragilis 63
R. langei 62
R. ochroleuca 53
R. parazurea 62
R. viriscens 53-54

Saffron Milk Cap 82-84
Saint George's Mushroom 86-87
Saprophytic fungi 17
Sautéing mushrooms 32
Scottish Outdoor Access Code 6
Shaggy Inkcap 84-86
Shaggy Parasol 79-80
Sparassis crispa 57-58
Spores 27
Spore print 27, 28
SSSI 6
Stem 29
Sulphur Tuft 90
Summer Truffle 88-89

Terracotta Hedgehog 69
Truffles 17
Trumpet Chanterelle 61-62
Trumpet of Death 71-72
Tuber aestivum 88-89

T. magnatum 89
T. melanosporum 89
Tubes 24

Velvet Shank 89-91
Vinegar Cup 75

Webcap 50
White Dapperling 68
White Truffle 89
Wild Mushroom Picker's Code of Conduct 6
The Wildlife Trust 14, 93
Winter Chanterelle 61-62
Wood Blewits 52-53
Wood Mushroom 67
Woodland Trust 93
Woolly Milk Cap 83

Yellow Legs 61
Yellow Staining Mushrooms 67, 73

Zygomycetes 20